The Dream Feed
Method

How we got our babies sleeping from
dusk till dawn. By month 4.
WITHOUT crying-it-out.

Jana's Well-Rested Moms and **Dads**
with
Jason Freedman and **Stacy Karol**
Brian Symon, M.D. and **Eileen Aicardi, M.D.**

The Dream Feed Method

Copyright © 2018 Jana Method LLC

ISBN (Print): 978-1-54393-237-9
ISBN (eBook): 978-1-54393-238-6

In memoriam of

Jana Hartzell

1968–2015

You Can Do This

You can get your baby happily sleeping from dusk till dawn by month four without crying-it-out.

When your baby sleeps well, you sleep well. When you sleep well, you get to be the parent you've always wanted to be. You will have the energy to fully love your baby, fully love your partner, and fully love yourself.

You can do this. We're going to help.

The Four Principles of the Dream Feed Method

1. Start in the First Four Months

2. Empower Your Partner to Use Top-Up Bottles

3. Preempt Crying with Dream Feeds

4. Dream Feed a Little Bit Earlier Each Night

Table of Contents

The Dream Feed Method: An Overview

1. Start in the First Four Months

Somewhere around the end of the fourth month, babies undergo a process called settling. They settle into a routine that imprints itself, becoming a baseline pattern that they will naturally gravitate to for the next several years. If around the four-month mark, your baby is getting up to feed twice a night, it will become increasingly hard to remove those two feedings. On the other hand, if she is no longer accustomed to additional nighttime feedings around the four-month mark, she'll be far less likely to demand them anytime in the future. Either way, the sleep and nighttime feeding pattern at the four-month mark is very sticky and difficult to change once it is set.

By doing the full Dream Feed Method before this settling occurs, you'll lock in a pattern of 12-hour sleeping, enabling you and your baby to skip crying-it-out altogether. Your baby never falls into an alternative pattern (such as feeding at 11:00 p.m. and 4:00 a.m.) that then becomes imprinted. And you avoid the hours of tears, surprise, and anger associated with removing an established pattern.

Start early, and it'll be easier for both you and your baby.

2. Empower Your Partner to Use Top-Up Bottles

The top-up bottle provides additional expressed breast milk (or formula) at night when the breasts have been drained but your baby is still hungry for more.

Let's say that the 7:00 p.m. feeding is the last feeding of the day before you'd like your baby to go down for the night. You'll breastfeed your baby for the typical amount of time—but, at the very end, you'll seamlessly transition to offering a bottle of expressed breast milk. Your baby shouldn't even notice that the nipples have been switched.

At first, she may only take half an ounce of extra milk. Over time, however, she'll start taking more and more top-up milk at this 7:00 p.m. feeding. These are the extra calories that will enable her to sleep much longer. With top-up bottles, your baby will more easily reach the first early milestone of going 3 hours between nighttime feedings.

Just as importantly, this is the beginning of getting your partner involved in the feedings. Top-up bottles and later dream feed bottles are an important way your partner can contribute to feeding and sleep training. And this helps Mom get longer stretches of sleep.

Empower your partner early on. For his benefit. For your benefit. And for your baby's benefit.

3. Preempt Crying with Dream Feeds

In the second month, or whenever your baby reaches 3 hours between nighttime feedings, you'll start to preempt the awakenings with dream feeds. This works whether you're co-sleeping, room-sharing, or have moved to separate rooms.

Go to your baby just before he is likely to wake up. If you're breastfeeding, you'll have to nudge him awake a little bit. But it still works! Your baby will be hungry enough that he will feed, even while mostly asleep.

If you're bottle-feeding, hold your baby upright but in a comfortable position for both of you. Take the nipple of the bottle and gently tickle his upper lip. Once your baby opens his mouth, gently slip the bottle in the open mouth and watch with amazement as he establishes a latch and starts sucking while still asleep!

Don't make any sounds or do anything other than let him drink the warm milk. With your baby still swaddled, stop about 70 percent through for a burp. If you absolutely must, do any changing you're going to do now. Try not to change wet diapers since the diaper and ointment are enough to prevent any rashes. And don't un-swaddle your baby just to check. Your goal is to avoid agitation. Return to feeding the remaining 30 percent or whatever else he is interested in taking. Try for one more burp. Put him down.

In the best of scenarios, your baby does not actually fully wake up. Once he finishes his last little bit of milk, put him back down and he'll settle back into sleep.

4. Dream Feed a Little Bit Earlier Each Night

The first three steps over the initial two months form a foundation that makes the Dream Feed Method possible. Now the magic begins.

Instead of simply hoping your baby sleeps a little longer with each feeding until you magically become the winner of the "my baby is a great sleeper" lottery, you're going to actively guide him. Each night you'll offer dream feeds *earlier* than the night before. This is where we diverge from virtually every other sleep-training method out there.

What does this look like? Let's say you're on a schedule where you start feeds at 7:00 p.m., 10:00 p.m., 1:00 a.m., 4:00 a.m., and then 7:00 a.m. That breaks the night into four distinct 3-hour sleeping periods.

You're going to lock in 7:00 a.m. as the first feeding of the day. The 4:00 a.m. feeding will become your "sliding feed"—moving earlier at small intervals. Your first step is moving that sliding feed back to 3:45 a.m. Because this is earlier than when he naturally wakes for his feeding, you're going to preempt any crying with a dream feed.

Following this, your baby has a full belly, is still swaddled tightly, and is probably asleep (or very close to it).

Now, you already know your baby is accustomed to going 3 hours— from 4:00 a.m. until the 7:00 a.m. feeding. By moving his dream feed earlier by just 15 minutes, you will find on the first morning that he wakes up exactly 3 hours later at 6:45 a.m.

Because 7:00 a.m. has been set as the first feed of the day, you'll hold off for those 15 minutes before feeding him. You can rock him, sing to him, bounce him, use a pacifier, or put him in a vibrating swing. Whatever works to keep him content. You just have to hold him off for 15 minutes before feeding him.

The shift of this "sliding feed" creates a domino effect. Moving the 4:00 a.m. feeding fifteen minutes earlier means you'll do the same to the other overnight feeds. Your feedings will now occur at 7:00 p.m., 9:45 p.m., 12:45 a.m., 3:45 a.m., and 7:00 a.m. You'll notice that this means the first sleep period is now only 2 hours and 45 minutes. The next two sleep periods remain exactly 3 hours. And the final sleep period has been *stretched backward* to 3 hours and 15 minutes.

You'll be surprised by how quickly your baby will adjust. When you've successfully reached 7:00 a.m. three days in a row without too much struggle, the pattern is set. This might not mean your baby is technically sleeping until 7:00 a.m. Success means he is content in his bassinet. Your baby has proven he can go from 3:45 a.m. to 7:00 a.m., and now you're ready to move that sliding feed another 15 minutes earlier. He'll likely never again demand a feeding between 3:45 a.m. and 7:00 a.m., which means that already you've avoided the dreaded 5:00 a.m. wake-up that plagues most parents for years.

You're going to keep stretching earlier throughout the night in 15-minute increments—waiting each time for your baby to prove to you that he can make it back to 7:00 a.m. without too much effort. Because you're shifting by such small increments, you will never need to let your baby cry for an extended period of time. Eventually, that first period of sleep will become condensed until it folds into the previous feeding and is therefore dropped altogether.

This is the magic. Every baby is different, but the chart here reflects a general schedule that is achievable for many babies. If your baby fits this pattern, sometime in the second month you can drop from three nighttime feedings to two nighttime feedings. You can be down to only one nighttime feeding in the third month. The goal is to be done with nighttime feedings by the end of the fourth month! Full dusk till dawn wonderful, quiet, restful sleep—without crying-it-out!

Dream Feed Method General Schedule

	7pm	8pm	9pm	10pm	11pm	12am	1am	2am	3am	4am	5am	6am	7am
Week 1	F+			zzz			zzz			zzz			F
Week 2	F+			zzz			zzz			zzz			F
Week 3	F+			zzz			zzz			zzz			F
Week 4	F+			zzz			zzz			zzz			F
Week 5	F+		zzz			zzz			zzz				F
Week 6	F+		zzz			zzz			zzz				F
Week 7	F+	zzz			zzz			zzz					F
Week 8	F+			zzz			zzz						F
Week 9	F+		zzz			zzz							F
Week 10	F+	zzz			zzz								F
Week 11	F+			zzz									F
Week 12	F+		zzz										F
Week 13	F+	zzz											F
Week 14	F+												F
Week 15	F+												F
Week 16	F+												F

F+   Feeding plus a Top-Up Bottle

F   Normal feeding when baby awakes (breast and/or bottle)

zzz   Dream Feed (breast and/or bottle)

PART 1:

Jana's Well-Rested Moms and Dads

Trust yourself.
You know more than you think you do.

—Dr. Spock

We Are Jana's Well-Rested Moms and Dads

We each first met Jana when we had our first baby. Since then, we've met and spoken with many of the parents who were lucky enough to have her in their lives. Some called her a night nanny, some called her a sleep trainer, and everyone agreed she was part 'baby whisperer.' We all called her family. We loved her for the immense patience, kindness, and warmth that she showered on our babies and on us.

On October 10, 2015, Jana tragically passed away.

This book is in her honor. It fulfills her wish that her effective sleep-training method be shared with mothers everywhere. Jana had such a lasting, important impact on each of us. Not only did she help us teach our babies to sleep through the night, she did so with a unique sense of calm and generosity that we all try to embody. It is in that very spirit that we've written this book.

While we hope this book teaches you everything you need to know about Jana's Dream Feed Method, we also hope you'll spend a moment getting to know the Jana that we loved so much. We have created the Jana Hartzell Foundation, and you can find more details about her life at www.dreamfeedmethod.com/janahartzell. We are donating profits from this book to the *Homeless Prenatal Program* in her honor.

With Love,
Jana's Well-Rested Moms and Dads!
Jason and Jen, Stacy and David, Laurie and Josh, Josh and Susan, Megan and Robert, Divya, Josie, Tana, Jeanne, Shirley, Nisha, Tanya, and many more!

Dear Moms

My name is Stacy. I'm one of the moms who put this book together.

Our son, Oliver, arrived six days after he was due—which meant my husband, Dave, and I were as 'ready' as any new parents could be. We'd taken the classes... we'd bought all of the 'things'... our freezer was full of home-cooked meals. And mentally, we'd been preparing for months, verbally managing one another's expectations, saying things like: "Our kitchen won't be this clean once the baby comes."

But in spite of our best efforts to *plan* and *prepare*, there were many things about being a new mother that surprised me. I knew I'd be too tired to *cook*—but it hadn't occurred to me that I might also be too tired to *eat*. I knew breastfeeding would be hard, but I couldn't have imagined those challenges would persist for weeks. And I'd heard that my hormones would do funny things to my mood, but nothing prepared me for the quantity of tears in those early weeks.

Yet, the thing that surprised me most had nothing to do with being a mother. Oliver's arrival had changed not just me, but my marriage as well. Dave and I had become like ships passing in the night.

Evenings of shared meals, conversation, and Netflix were replaced by strategic games of 'divide and conquer' (read: I slept with earplugs in, while he walked the halls with our wailing infant).

I now look back on those early weeks with a sigh and a smile. Starting when Oliver was four weeks old, Dave and I jointly committed our little family to The Dream Feed Method. What followed were six weeks of teamwork like I'd never before experienced in my marriage. It turned out that teaching our baby how to sleep through the night brought us closer as a married couple and set us on a path of unique equality as parents.

To be sure, our path to 'Dusk till Dawn' was not without a few bumps and curves. There was the occasional 1:00 a.m. heated debate at the changing table, our wide-awake two-month-old watching us curiously. There were strings of 2, 3, and 4 nights where I was sure the Dream Feed Method simply would not work for *our* baby. We stayed the course, however, and by ten weeks Oliver was sleeping from 6:30 p.m. to 6:30 a.m. And that routine has remained largely consistent.

Something else that has remained consistent is our spirit of equal partnership. While co-navigating The Dream Feed Method, Dave and I built a confidence as parents that now flows into every corner of our family life.

Whether you're expecting your first or your fourth, my wish is that you too will experience the benefits of not only a good night's sleep, but also everything that comes with that. Motherhood is a journey, for sure. Let those first twelve weeks set the tone for a lifetime of partnership.

With Love,
Stacy Karol

Dear Dads

My name's Jason. I'm married to Jen, and we have three wonderful children, Alex, Callie, and Ethan. Having now talked to hundreds of dads, I want to share two observations:

First, most first-time dads have no idea about sleep training before becoming a parent. They attend classes on supporting their wife in labor, infant care, infant CPR, and first aid. But nothing on sleep training.

Second, most dads say that they would have become way more involved in sleep training earlier had they known more about it. But when they did learn, it felt too late.

When I talk to dads around the six-month mark, they're tired. Their wives are tired. Their babies are tired. And they're trying to figure out why they weren't lucky enough to have a baby who magically sleeps through the night. They're disappointed to learn that there were steps that they could have easily taken to put their families on a better track. And while there are steps that they can still take, such as using the "cry-it-out" method, those options seem far from appealing.

I was fortunate enough to receive some valuable advice from a dear friend before we had our first baby. He said, "It's all well and good to spend so much time learning about what to do in the first week. But if I can recommend one area where you can really make a difference...it's sleep training. I know this woman, Jana; you should really talk to her. She'll teach you more about sleep training than you'd ever thought you'd know."

Dads, I just want to tell you how much your role in this process matters. I know from experience that prioritizing a full and peaceful night's sleep for both my baby AND my wife has made all of the difference in our day-to-day happiness. I encourage you to put sleep training right up there on your project to-do list, alongside installing the car seat and putting together the nursery furniture.

I work full-time and, like many dads, didn't get much paternity leave. I know how hard it is to balance nighttime feedings and a full workday. But I promise: if you commit to playing a role in sleep training your baby during these crucial first few months, you, your wife, and your baby will get far more rest for years to come.

I knew Jana well, and I'm the one that most encouraged her to write a book about the Dream Feed Method. After her passing, I spent a couple of years interviewing all her moms, recruiting Dr. Aicardi and Dr. Symon, and helping to pull together this book. It's been a wonderful journey and a pleasure to honor Jana by furthering her mission: helping more parents and their babies get a good night's sleep.

If you're waiting for your first child, I will tell you fatherhood is the absolute best. You're going to love it. And if you ever lose that perspective, I'm willing to bet it's because you're sleep deprived. I hope this book helps you in the same way Jana's wisdom helped me.

Most Sincerely,
Jason Freedman

Meet Eileen Aicardi, M.D.

Hello Parents,

I'm Dr. Aicardi. I first became interested in the Dream Feed Method when Jason and Jen, parents I've watched raise three kids, came to ask me to be an advisor. Jana had recently passed away, and they wanted an active pediatrician to provide a perspective in the book. Of course, I love the opportunity to talk about something I'm so passionate about: helping the entire family be healthy and well-rested.

I am first and foremost a mom. When I was younger, I had years of infertility, so we chose to adopt. Just before our adopted son was born, I found out

I was pregnant. The adoption went through as planned, and the pregnancy stuck. We had two wonderful boys, born seven months apart.

Then I had a baby naturally seventeen months after number two. That's three wonderful boys in 24 months.

After I stopped nursing number three, my period never came. Guess what? I was pregnant with identical twins. They were born thirteen months after my third.

I have five wonderful boys born within 38 months. My hair is very gray.

And I've been in practice as a pediatrician for 40 years. I've seen thousands of babies. Now I have the privilege of taking care of my "grandchildren," the children of children I took care of in my practice years ago.

I don't claim to know what's best for you, and your own consultation with your pediatrician should always come first. Ultimately, the parent always gets to decide. This is just a book with advice. It's your baby, it's your night, and it's your sleep.

Warmest Regards,
Eileen Aicardi, M.D.

Meet Brian Symon, M.D.

Dear Parents,

My patients have dubbed me "The Sleep Doctor." I have been caring for families with young children for upwards of 40 years. As soon as I read a working draft of the Dream Feed Method, I wanted to be involved. I knew that it would support parental well-being and that it would dramatically decrease infant crying in the early days and weeks of life.

In my professional work, I care for two types of clinical presentations: sleep problem avoidance and sleep problem resolution. This book is all about sleep problem avoidance. The Dream Feed Method recommends focusing on the nutritional needs of a newborn, which in today's world are too often overlooked. It is a statement of practical reality that a hungry baby will not sleep.

I count it a privilege to have been able to contribute to this book and congratulate all of Jana's Well-Rested Moms and Dads for shouldering a task that has become a labor of love. To the parents who read this book, I wish you every success in your parenting journey. There is only one reason to become a parent: the joy of parenting. May every day with your baby be a joy.

As a father of four with my eldest now approaching 50 years, I can assure you that every age has its pleasures. As I write these words, I am home caring for our 3-year-old grandson who is fast asleep. Children are so easy to love when they sleep.

Best wishes to you and your family.
Brian Symon, M.D.

Dr. Symon is the author of two books:

Silent Nights: Overcoming Sleep Problems in Babies and Children

Your Baby Manual: For Optimal Sleep, Feeding and Growth in Babies and Children

And many peer-reviewed studies, including:

"Effect of a Consultation Teaching Behavior Modification on Sleep Performance in Infants: A Randomized Controlled Trial," published in the *The Medical Journal of Australia*.

"INFANT SLEEP DISORDERS. THEIR SIGNIFICANCE AND EVIDENCE-BASED STRATEGIES FOR PREVENTION. A RANDOMIZED CONTROLLED TRIAL," published in the *The Medical Journal of Australia*.

"THE JOY OF PARENTING: INFANT SLEEP INTERVENTION TO IMPROVE MATERNAL EMOTIONAL WELL-BEING AND INFANT SLEEP," published in the *The Singapore Medical Journal*.

What It Means to Be a Well-Rested Mom

Are you nervous about having a baby? So were we.

What specifically are you nervous about? Is it the responsibility of nurturing, caring for, protecting, and ultimately providing for this tiny person? Is it wondering whether you're ready, or whether you'll ever be? Is it having enough money? Is it having enough space?

And, on top of all that, are you just worried about being tired—all the time?

You know the type of person you become when you're tired. Irritable. Impatient. Unreasonable. Are you nervous about being that person all the time? To address this universal anxiety, let us paint you a "what if" picture.

What if we could assure you that within four months of giving birth to your child, your baby will sleep peacefully from dusk till dawn? That without using the cry-it-out method or any traumatizing sleep-training techniques, your baby will be happily, peacefully, consistently asleep for 12 hours every night?

At 7:00 p.m., you'll put your baby down, and she'll put herself to sleep within a few minutes. You won't feed, soothe, or listen to cries until 7:00 a.m. the next morning.

Your friends with kids may have already scared you with stories of getting up two or three times a night for the first 18 months. But what if your experience could be different?

What would it mean for your life, your marriage, and the well-being of your baby?

1. You will get your evenings back.

The bedtime ritual is only going to take a few minutes; at 7:00 p.m., you're done—the evening is yours. You could enjoy dinner with your spouse, read a book, and watch a movie. You'll have time and energy for romance. Anything you currently do now between 7:00 p.m. and whatever your current bedtime is will still be your time. This time period will not change pre- and post-baby. So, you can continue your hobbies or work late or devour your favorite novels. You can continue the quality time you currently enjoy with your partner. Every single evening will effectively be a 'night off.'

2. You can hire babysitters.

In fact, it's going to be the easiest babysitting job they've ever had. You invite them to come over at 7:00 p.m., and the baby is already put to sleep. Their job is literally to sit there, do their homework, and make sure a fire doesn't start in the house. You can go out and see friends after 7:00 p.m., or have a weekly date night, or do whatever you want without even having to trust the babysitter to put the baby down.

But it's also fine to teach your babysitter how to put your baby down because, frankly, it's not going to be a complicated affair. If it takes you 20 minutes to put your baby to sleep, it's going to take your babysitter 20 minutes as well.

3. You can take nights away.

Because your baby sleeps through the night and is easy to put down at night, it should be totally fine for you to leave for the weekend after the first four months. Have your parents come over for the weekend, and they're going to be able to enjoy their grandchild from 7:00 a.m.

to 7:00 p.m. And at 7:00 p.m., they get to call it a night and get their own rest.

Because your baby is so easy to care for, you can leave for a weekend, guilt-free. Go to that wedding. Or that reunion. Or just take a weekend at the spa together. Plan on doing something fun, not just restful. Because you're sleeping fully every night, it's not like you're going to need to catch up on sleep during your vacation. Plan fun things with your spouse just like you did when you were dating. You'll have plenty of energy for it and will come back even more energized and reconnected.

4. You will get your mornings back.

If you're the type who likes to wake up early and work out, schedule that every day of the week if you choose. One parent needs to be home at all times for safety, but there's no reason why one of you can't work out for an hour every morning. It'll do wonders for how you feel, and because your baby is sleeping soundly until 7:00 a.m. there's nothing to do in the morning anyway. On the mornings you're not working out, enjoy a leisurely cup of coffee and make yourself a nice breakfast. Read the paper. Mornings should be relaxed until your baby wakes up at 7:00 a.m. and is ready for her first feeding of the day.

5. You will get your energy back.

You're not going to be irritable, impatient, or unreasonable. In fact, you should have even more energy than you did before the baby was born, when you had the added responsibility of being pregnant. Yes, absolutely, you'll be tired during the first few months while you're working through the Dream Feed Method. But from the fourth month onward, you'll have the energy to go back to tackling your job or simply engaging with the people around you. Exhaustion won't play a primary role in your life.

6. Your marriage will get its energy back.

Because you won't be so exhausted, you'll treat your partner with the level of care that you always have up until this point. You won't take out your exhaustion on each other. You won't fight over small things, because you'll have the energy to remember that small things are indeed small. You won't consider your partner like a fellow employee at a sweatshop where you're both working past the point of your physical capacity. You'll get to spend quality time together—just the two of you.

7. And best of all, you will get a happier, healthier, less-fussy baby.

Your baby is going to sleep 12 hours a night, from dusk till dawn. In this first year of her life, sleeping well is one of the greatest gifts you can possibly give her. You'll give her body and brain all of this extra, uninterrupted rest in order to do the hard work of growing. You'll notice how happy and peaceful your baby is during the day. If you thought all babies were fussy, you'll be surprised to find out that most fussiness is caused by lack of quality sleep.

Because your baby sleeps a full 12 hours every night, she'll wake up in a great mood and spend the day in a great mood. You'll spend less time trying to calm her down. And with a great nighttime sleep schedule, it will also be much easier to have a great daytime sleep schedule. You will be happy to know that this added rest has been proven to lead to better brain development, which is scientifically correlated with higher IQ and fewer mental disorders later in life.

What was it again that you were so worried about? Parenthood is fabulous. You're going to love having this little bundle of joy. Take a deep breath.

Your baby is going to sleep, and so will you. You can do this.

What It Means To Be a Well-Rested Dad

Yes, this book is also for you, dads and partners. You, too, dread sleepless nights, low energy, and loss of personal time for you and your marriage. Everything that was a benefit for Mom in the last section is obviously also a benefit for you. But as the one who did not carry this baby for nine months, who did not endure hours of labor and weeks of recovery, as the one who did not have her entire body altered in order to sustain another human being, you may believe that the responsibilities of sleep training don't fall on your shoulders.

You could not be more wrong.

Your role as a full participant in the Dream Feed Method will have the biggest impact on whether it will be successful. While this method talks about scheduled breastfeeding, nipple confusion, top-up bottles, replacement bottles, and so many other tactics, this entire strategy could be rephrased as this: Empower Dad to do 50 percent of the nighttime feedings.

It's true: Mom's buy-in to the process is essential. Lots of research has shown that the mother is usually the gatekeeper to important decisions about the care of a newborn, but if your wife is encouraging you to read this book, you're being given the opportunity to be significantly involved in this process. And while it will be a lot of work, it will be one of the most meaningful contributions you can make to your baby's first few months of life, your wife's well-being, and the happiness of your entire family. Jump right in with both feet. It's well worth it.

Here are just a few additional benefits of becoming a well-rested dad.

1. You bond with your new baby much earlier.

No father wants to admit that they feel anything less than absolute love for their newborn baby, but the unspoken reality is that moms and dads have a very different relationship in the beginning. Moms have spent 9+ months carrying this baby inside them, feeling every kick and turn, aware of hiccups and sleep. After giving birth, mother and baby bond with skin-to-skin contact in the early relationship of breastfeeding. Meanwhile, the dads are often the ones rushing around to move the bags, fill the water bottles, change the diapers, and do the burping. They easily become servants to the process and the environment, with less opportunity to just enjoy intimate bonding with their newborn.

No matter what the perspective of the mother is and no matter what the perspective of the father is, the differences between the way that mothers and fathers attempt to bond with their baby early on are somewhat inevitable, if for no other reason than the breastfeeding mom spends a lot more time with her baby close to her. This is one of the most powerful benefits of being able to give the responsibility for a top-up bottle and one replacement bottle to the dad early in the process. You will find, dads, that your 7:00 p.m. top-up bottle will be one of your favorite times to sit alone with your newborn. You will probably enjoy the middle of the night dream feeds a little less, but I guarantee you'll never forget those moments. They will mean more to you, since you were not just retrieving a crying baby and delivering him to your wife, but actually fulfilling his need by feeding and soothing him back to sleep.

2. Sharing sleep-training responsibility will give you a much better relationship with your wife.

For absolutely every single couple out there, having a newborn baby is hard—massively, massively hard. There are thousands of tiny decisions, not all of which you both agree on. The responsibility for this new life is unending. You lose your own personal time and the space to take care of yourself—and you do all this while sleep deprived. Even in the strongest marriages, it's incredibly stressful.

The role a dad gets to play in the Dream Feed Method will be a gift to your marriage, and not just because everyone will be getting to a full night's sleep sooner—though, let's be clear, that is by far the biggest benefit. Before the full nights of sleep even happen, you're going to be sharing in both the effort and the benefits of sleep training... right from the beginning. When you take over a nighttime feeding, you also enable your wife to sleep through it. In doing this, your appreciation for each other will only grow.

3. Your baby will be happier and healthier.

New dads are often searching for any possible way to make their baby just a little bit safer, healthier, and happier. Playing a role in sleep training early on is absolutely something to add to that list, and it has such a profound effect on your baby. As you help your baby lengthen the time he spends asleep each night, you'll notice a direct correlation to his daytime moods: he'll spend less time being fussy, which means you get to enjoy more moments. And you will know that you were instrumental in achieving this.

4. Sleep training is truly fascinating.

This will be one of the parts of parenthood that you really get into. Most dads that participate in the Dream Feed Method end up becoming experts in all sleep-training subjects. You'll be surprised how often you find yourself excitedly talking about sleep training with other dads. While moms generally struggle to find a way to talk to each other when their philosophies differ, dads often don't face this barrier. In fact, you absolutely should talk with as many of your fellow new dads as possible, both to learn what's working for them and to share what's working for you. Every baby may be unique, but the empathy shared between dads is universal.

5. You can give your wife the (long-term) gift of sleep.

Many moms who don't do the Dream Feed Method can go months, even years without a full night's rest, and they lose something of themselves in the process. When you give your wife the ability to get a full night's rest, especially early on, you give her the gift of rejuvenation, and you'll see in her the woman you love, unburdened by what had seemed like unending sleep deprivation.

6. You give the gift of sleep to yourself.

Make no bones about it. The Dream Feed Method asks that the partners be more involved in sleep training. That means that during these crucial first few months you will absolutely be up more at night than other dads. That's no small imposition when you've probably already resumed your day job. But here's the really good news: the interrupted nights are going to end much sooner. Your involvement will play a huge role in successfully getting your baby to sleep not just what other parents call "through the night," which is often just 5 or 6 hours, but actually fully from dusk till dawn.

That means four months from now, you won't be listening to your baby cry at 4:00 a.m. Six months from now you won't be staying up until 10:00 or 11:00 p.m. to sneak in an additional feeding. Nine months from now, you won't be canceling your weekend plans in order to give cry-it-out a third chance. Twelve months from now, you won't be dreading that trip to your parents' because you know it will ruin your kids' fragile sleep patterns. A little bit of hard work now is going to pay dividends every night for years. Don't fall into the trap of thinking you don't have a role in this. You absolutely do.

Don't underestimate the impact of having a newborn to your own well-being. Don't underestimate the stress you endure. Don't underestimate how your own body falls apart when sleep deprived. Don't underestimate the value of having a rested, healthy family—not just for their sake, but also for your own. You want to be the one who has limitless patience. You want to be the one who never tires of time with your family. You want to be the one with enough energy to exercise, work, play, think, socialize, love, and more.

Being a full participant in helping your baby sleep from dusk till dawn is the greatest gift you can give yourself. And so we say to you the same thing that we say to the moms: You can do this. We're going to help.

A Dad's Perspective: My Job Was Taking Care of My Wife

I think dads are told by virtually everyone that in the early days they are only really responsible for one thing: changing diapers. You're pretty much off the hook for everything else. But I would say that sleep training is an essential thing you can do incredibly well, a thing that will make two people in your life extremely happy: your wife and your baby—well, three, if you count yourself!

I didn't love getting up at 4:00 a.m., but I did love being able to feed the baby with a bottle. Bonus: my wife woke up feeling better rested, which meant a better mood.

I think if they realized they could use a bottle in the middle of the night, most dads would do it. I just don't think many dads know that they can or feel like they're allowed to.

Emily was so focused on taking care of our baby that someone needed to take care of her. There are things you can do to take care of your wife, things that no one else is going to do. She won't do it for herself. Someone had to come in and say, 'I'm going to reserve a little piece of you that you get to keep for yourself,' and if that meant giving her an extra 3 hours of sleep every night, that's what it was. She wasn't going to do it for herself. It had to come from me.

—Joel (Dad of two)

Pick the One Sleep-training Philosophy That's Right for You

There is no one-size-fits-all approach. There is no right and wrong. There is no good parenting and bad parenting. Sleep training, like all other parenting decisions, is about making the best decision you can. If, in the end, you and your baby sleep a little less or a little more, you'll both still be fine.

You're going to be fine, because you're a parent. You're going to make the decision that's right for you. No person on the planet has the right to tell you how to parent your child. Love your child with the very best of intentions. Try to do what's right. Try with all your might to block out everyone who tells you otherwise.

Amongst the group of us who wrote *The Dream Feed Method*, we instinctually fall on different points of the spectrum between attachment parenting and the sleep trainers.

We love breastfeeding but it's not a 100% of the time absolute. We love cuddling our babies, but not all the time. We hate listening to our babies cry. We hate being told not to soothe our own babies. We also don't want to be up several times a night for the first year and beyond. We want our babies to rest peacefully, on their own. We understand that crying-it-out may work, but we would rather not do it if possible, because really, who wants to hear their baby cry for hours?

We also remember the joy of being pregnant with our first babies and not knowing that such a philosophical fight over how to raise your baby loomed on the horizon. And we remember being surprised to see how divisive this conversation is, especially online.

We remember how disconcerting it was when this conversation became divisive amongst our friends and family, many of whom felt it was their obligation to share their opinions on how we should raise our babies.

The Dream Feed Method is one of many decisions that you two will make as parents about how to raise your child, regardless of how others try to influence you with their unsolicited advice.

Here are some of the main tenets over which many in the 'baby advice' community disagree and where The Dream Feed Method stands.

Co-sleeping/Room-sharing/Separate Room

We believe anything goes in the first month; pick what's right for you. By the second or third month, we lean towards independent sleeping in a different room, but we're not religious about it. For those parents that follow the appropriate safety precautions, we don't believe that there is a substantial difference in safety for any of the options. We do believe it's generally easier to find success with The Dream Feed Method the earlier you move towards independent sleep in a separate room. But because you can get there irrespective of which decision you make, we simply refuse to hold a strong opinion about this.

On-Demand Feeding/Scheduled Feeding

For the first month, do whatever you like. In those first few weeks, on-demand feeding is totally fine. Once your baby has gained back her birth weight and is growing nicely, start moving toward scheduled feedings. Aim to get to scheduled feedings by around the second month for most full-term babies.

Parent-soothing/Self-soothing

We don't actually care that much about this subject. We believe that babies cry the most when they're hungry, so the Dream Feed Method places a lot of emphasis on feeding babies more at night. Less-hungry babies cry less, and babies who aren't crying don't present this intractable question of whether to soothe or to not soothe. Our favorite part of The Dream Feed Method is that they learn self-soothing AND there is no focus on letting them cry.

When Breast is Best or Fed is Best

Breastfeeding is best. Most of the time. When it works. And when it doesn't work, supplementing with expressed breast milk from a bottle is fine. And when there's not enough, supplementing with some formula is fine, too. Set the breastfeeding goal for yourself that works for you, and don't be afraid to supplement your goal with bottles and formula. We focus on ensuring that the baby is fully fed. So, we encourage you to tone down the pressure you put on yourself to exclusively breastfeed.

When it comes to sleep-training methodologies that all seem to be at odds with each other, make the decision that's right for you and your family.

You can do this. With or without our help.

A Mom's Perspective:
Visualize What Type of Parent You Want to Be

In the beginning, Ben and I took some time to visualize. (We're big on that in my family.) What's our vision for our family and for our unborn baby and for the kind of parents we want to be?

Early on, we recognized that if we're happy people, then we're probably happily married. If we're happily married, then our baby is going to do great. If he's got two parents who love each other and he's living in a home that's well-rested and happy and healthy and full of love, then he's going to be doing great, too.

For us, sleep is one of the first steps to staying happy.

Sleep became the foundation for so much. Now we both have energy to exercise. I started running again a couple of weeks ago. I could not do that if I was waking up four times a night. Ben is doing well at work; when he comes home, he's happy and we're able to have a conversation. I'll go back to work in a few months and know that I can bring my best self to both my family and my career.

—Sarah (Mom of a four-month-old)

Read This Book Before Giving Birth

There are a thousand things to think about before you give birth to your baby; especially if this is your first baby.

You have the baby registry and the nursery. The obstetrician check-ups and ultrasounds. Hospitals to tour. Labor classes, infant CPR classes, and introduction to parenthood classes. Maybe you're switching jobs or moving. Or packing in those last few international trips you've been wanting to take.

We know you're busy.

But every night you go to sleep whenever you want to sleep, and every morning you wake up fully rested. Right now is when you have plenty of energy to absorb new information, talk with your partner, and create a vision for what you want in your soon-to-be-growing family.

Create for yourself a vision of a well-rested baby who peacefully sleeps from dusk till dawn.

Create for yourself a vision of a well-rested family, with both you and your partner at your best.

And create for yourself a vision of *you* as a well-rested mom. Because when your baby sleeps well, you will sleep well.

Parenthood will still be hard—there will always be a thousand things to think about. But create for yourself a vision of you at your best taking it on. Not just surviving, but actually thriving.

You can do this. And this little bit of preparation will be instrumental in helping you get there.

PART 2:

Why the Dream Feed Method

People who say they sleep like a baby don't have one.

—Leo J. Burke

1. Why Start in the First Four Months

Your Baby Can Sleep from Dusk till Dawn

Of all the great tips and tricks unlocked by the Dream Feed Method, this little tidbit of information is perhaps more powerful than anything else: your baby is physically capable of sleeping from dusk till dawn, 12 hours in a row, within the first four months.

By preempting crying with dream feeds, you're teaching your baby to sleep longer and longer periods without the discomfort of crying-it-out. Frankly, using dream feeds is just easier both on your baby and on you. Relative to most other sleep-training methods out there, it's not that hard to do, so there's no reason not to start earlier.

Additionally, top-up bottles ensure that your baby has plenty to eat. Not only are you guaranteeing that he will start with a full feeding at 7:00 p.m., but your baby learns to take in more than a full feeding to sleep through the night. He will also learn to take in more milk during the day.

With both dream feeds and top-up bottles at your disposal, it's possible to start sleep training much earlier than other parents do. Not only is it possible, it's necessary, as we discuss in the next section.

A Researcher's Perspective: Aim for Ten to Twelve Hours by Three Months

I try to encourage children to be sleeping between ten and twelve hours in an unbroken block at night by three months of age. The majority of children can achieve this target, with guidance.

—Brian Symon, M.D.

A Mom's Perspective: Our Doctor Was Happy as Long as Our Son Gained Weight

When we went into the doctor's office for the three-month checkup, she asked how sleep was going. We said, "Great. He's sleeping through the night." She said, "Terrific. Like six to eight hours?" We answered, "No, twelve."

Her reply was, "Wow, that's amazing. Good job!" Then we moved on to the next thing. She was surprised, I think, by the number of hours he was sleeping, but there seemed to be no concern about him not eating for that block of time.

As long as the weight gain trajectory was healthy, I realized the doctor would not be too concerned about the length of time between feeds. He was gaining plenty of weight. He was growing in the same percentile. He was mapping the trajectory that she wanted to see him follow.

Because he was healthy in all other regards, sleeping 12 hours was a non-issue, from our doctor's perspective.

—Megan (Mom of one)

Start Before Your Baby Settles

Two things happen somewhere around the end of the fourth month that make it essential that you have completed your sleep-training process before then. The first is that babies undergo a process called settling.

They settle into a routine that imprints itself; a routine that becomes a baseline pattern to which they will naturally gravitate. The baby's brain is, of course, undergoing development, and this early sleep milestone sticks as a difficult-to-alter pattern after the fourth month.

By doing the full Dream Feed Method before this settling occurs, you'll lock in this pattern of 12-hour sleeping. While it's certainly possible to be effective later, it will never be locked-in in the same way. Babies that don't successfully reach full dusk till dawn sleeping before the end of the fourth month are more prone to infamous sleep regressions, whereas babies that successfully complete the sleep-training process before the end of the fourth month seem almost impervious to these relapses.

By completely dodging the pitfalls of future sleep regressions, you'll experience greater flexibility throughout your child's early years. You can change time zones or have grandma visit. Your baby can get sick or weather the arrival of a new molar. None of it will seem to disrupt the 12-hour sleep cycle as long as it was imprinted early.

The second powerful reason to start early is that it helps your baby learn good sleep and self-soothing habits before a different set of patterns settles in. Babies that still receive nighttime feeds at five, six, seven months (and beyond!) will learn that when they wake at night, they must be fed in order to fall back to sleep. Because your baby will still be quite young when he no longer needs these middle of the night feeds, you won't ever need to teach him this (typically in the form of cry-it-out). Instead, your baby will naturally learn to put himself back to sleep as long as his other nighttime associations are present.

Finally, there's one additional, wonderful reason to start much, much earlier than most parents do. When you start the Dream Feed Method right from the beginning, that period of parental exhaustion is far briefer, only lasting for about eight weeks.

While the Dream Feed Method in full can take up to four months, the hardest part starts even earlier. It is absolutely doable to be back to sleeping 8 hours per night by the third month.

Not only is starting early a necessity for the Dream Feed Method to work, it's also its greatest gift.

A Pediatrician's Perspective:
Start at the End of the First Month

By the end of the first month and into the second month, most babies start to define daytime differently than nighttime. In daytime, they're more awake, and they start to sleep better at night.

This doesn't mean they sleep all night, but when they do wake up they recognize it's not time to play. They eat, and then they're eager to get back to sleep.

—Eileen Aicardi, M.D.

But What if My Baby Is a Bad Sleeper?

Some babies are more naturally inclined to longer stretches of sleep. The concept of a baby's temperament is real. However, it just doesn't matter as much as many parents think it does.

Consider this: while some kids may learn to read earlier and more easily, we don't discount those who might pick it up more slowly. Of course, everyone can learn how to read, even if some may have to work at it a little bit more.

The same goes for sleep training. Every baby can learn how to sleep from dusk till dawn in the first four months. Some may just need a bit more help than others. Try not to classify your baby as an "easy baby" or a "hard baby." Instead, focus on teaching her and trust that she has the capacity to learn.

There is some very interesting research that backs this up.

Researchers Teresa Pinilla and Leann Birch from the University of Illinois set out to answer the age-old question of nature versus nurture when it comes to sleep training. (See their article, "Help Me Make It through the Night: Behavioral Entrainment of Breast-fed Infants' Sleep Patterns.")

The study recruited a group of first-time parents who intended to breastfeed their babies and had complication-free pregnancies. They were split into two groups: Treatment and Control. Both groups were asked to meet with a practitioner weekly after giving birth.

When the babies in the Treatment group were three weeks old and had passed their normal health and weight milestones, the study's practitioners suggested to the parents that they "lengthen the latency of feeding time in the middle of the night" and provided them with instructions on how to stretch nighttime feedings.

The Control group received the exact same amount of interaction with the same practitioners, but the practitioners omitted the sleep-training advice. Both groups were asked to rate their babies' sleep temperaments as well as keep sleep diaries for two months.

At eight weeks, 100 percent of infants in the Treatment group were sleeping 6+ hours, compared with 23 percent in the Control group.

Total milk intake and weight gain for both groups was nearly identical. Infants in the Treatment group consumed more milk in the morning, and infants in the Control group consumed more milk in the night.

The conclusions from this study were pretty clear. Even a small amount of standard sleep-training advice had a significant effect on the infants in the Treatment group. If temperament were such a large factor, you would expect to see more variation within each group. While some infants did begin sleeping through the night earlier in each group, the far more important factor for the infants was whether their parents chose to implement sleep-training techniques.

Just because it doesn't come easily to your baby, doesn't mean he can't learn how to sleep. The beauty of the Dream Feed Method is that it allows you to build upon small wins. Persistence in sleep training will pay off. Even the toughest of babies can sleep from dusk till dawn by the fourth month.

A Pediatrician's Perspective:
Every Baby's Different. I Understand That.

I do think, though, that there are steps and ways that all parents can help move their babies toward sleeping for longer stretches. The number of babies for whom nothing works is very small. But what does happen as the whole sleeping issue gets more and more ingrained in the family dynamics is that it gets harder and harder to impact change.

—Eileen Aicardi, M.D.

A Mom's Perspective: If Our Baby Could Do It...

If there were a baby that would not have worked with this method, or any method, it would be ours.

He had feeding issues and he was not a good sleeper—up multiple times a night. It took him forever to get to 12 pounds. It seemed like we were struggling with him so much more than any of the other parents in my Mommy and Me class.

What we learned was that our baby was a "bad sleeper" because he was a bad eater. He would snack during the day and at night. Once we got to 3 hours between feedings during the day, we realized that a bottle for the dream feed would be better for him. It took less time and effort for him to get more milk in the middle of the night than breastfeeding. Making sure he was getting a full feed was the key to making this method work without crying.

And guess what? By the end of those three and a half months, he was the only baby in our Mommy and Me class who slept 12 hours a night.

It was hard. But it works. We didn't do anything special. Just working our way through this book, we went from having the fussiest baby who never slept to a healthy, growing baby who sleeps 12 straight hours. And we never had to suffer through cry-it-out.

—Emily

Good Sleepers Get You the First Six Hours

Okay. Yes. There absolutely is a difference between good sleepers and bad sleepers.

Yes, they're born that way.

Yes, it's the luck of the draw.

Talk to any parent of multiple kids, and you will rarely find consistency amongst how their kids slept.

Some are fussier than others. Some fall asleep easier on their own. Some stay asleep easier on their own. Some have adorable little whimpering cries, and some have bellowing wails.

One of the unfortunate results of too many sleep-training books is that they all seem to purposefully exert a sense of guilt onto the parents. As a result, the parents of good sleepers feel like it was their efforts alone that developed their good sleeper, and the parents of bad sleepers feel like they're just doing whatever they can to survive.

The reality is that both are true: babies are born with different temperaments *and* parents' sleep-training decisions matter. No parents whose baby sleeps from dusk till dawn did so on temperament alone, but it sure helps, and it specifically helps in achieving the first 6 hours of sleep.

Nearly all babies, even the most difficult sleepers, eventually get to at least a 6-hour stretch. The good sleepers, born with an easy temperament, can get there as early as the first few weeks without any significant intervention on behalf of the parents. The tougher babies may take several months to get there, if left to their own devices.

One of the benefits of the Dream Feed Method is that we help the parents of easy babies lock in those wins and progress quickly to a full dusk till dawn sleeping pattern, and we help the parents of the tougher babies coach their fussy sleepers without resorting to cry-it-out. It's easier for the first group, and because of that, they should bite their tongue and withhold judgment. For the latter group, just know that many of us also had very tough babies. We know it's not easy, but we can't say it enough: You can do this.

A Pediatrician's Perspective: There Is No Such Thing as a Newborn Baby Sleeping Too Long

If a baby is gaining weight, there's no such thing as sleeping too long. There are babies who will go 8 hours in the first month. Even more will go 8 hours by two months. That's not too long if they're gaining weight.

They make up for it the rest of the day. They're hungrier during the waking hours. What you're trying to do is teach them that eating happens during the day when you're awake and that nighttime is for sleeping.

And don't worry about milk production. The idea is to follow the baby's lead. If your baby is sleeping, you should sleep, too. Restorative sleep will do more for you and your milk production than anything else possibly could. If mothers do wake up and their breasts are really uncomfortable, then I tell them to express enough for comfort so they can go back to sleep. But don't purposely wake yourself up to pump a full feeding.

As babies learn to sleep all night, mothers just don't make milk at night. They wake up in the morning with full breasts. Their bodies naturally begin to adapt to whatever the pattern the baby needs, including having a longer stretch at night. Your body will adapt to it. Let it.

—Eileen Aicardi, M.D.

Starting Early Prevents Sleep Regressions Later

Crying-it-out to solve a sleep regression is the absolute worst. You'll have your heart ripped right out of you. You'll wonder what you could have done differently. Maybe you shouldn't have gone to see the grandparents. Maybe you should have been more diligent that time you had friends over. Maybe you should have left stricter instructions when you went away on that weekend for your anniversary.

For most parents, these regressions occur when the baby was never fully sleep trained before four months. If a baby is sleep trained after the fourth month, it's too late for the habit to become imprinted permanently. For the next few years, that baby's sleep will be fragile; thus, the parents will lead fragile lives. They'll be nervous about taking trips or leaving the baby overnight with babysitters or grandparents. They'll be incredibly vigilant about daytime naps, scheduling their lives around making sure they stick to the routine because of an intense fear of sleep regressions.

With the Dream Feed Method, once we successfully reach the dusk till dawn sleep habit in the first four months, the sleep training is locked in.

We tell mothers after they successfully make it to 12 hours to go back to enjoying life. If they want to take a trip, they can take a trip. The baby's going to change time zones easily. She'll still get her 12 hours of sleep. If they want to leave for three days and have the grandparents watch her, that's fine, too. They can't really mess anything up because the baby's sleep patterns are locked in.

Don't worry too much about disrupting the daytime nap schedule. If you have a fun afternoon with friends, and you want to keep your daughter out

2 hours past her normal naptime, it's no big deal. She's still going to go to sleep at 7:00 p.m. that night and wake up at 7:00 a.m. the next morning.

You don't get an unlimited pass to be reckless with your child's schedule. But if you do push it too far, you'll be able to fix it fairly easily by returning to consistency. There should never be a time that you have to cry-it-out.

To implement the Dream Feed Method, you have to be incredibly disciplined during the first four months, much more disciplined than your friends who aren't going to start sleep training until later. But your vigilance to do sleep training early and fully means that you've bought yourself a lot of flexibility for the next few years. It's an investment that pays back many, many, many times over.

A Researcher's Perspective:
Patterns Set at Four Months Last Five Years

For the thriving baby, a nighttime sleep of this length can be achieved before 4 months of age. This establishes a nighttime sleep pattern for the child for the next five or six years. Once sleeping from 7:00 p.m. to 7:00 a.m., the child should keep that pattern until school age. This is another landmark in that it gives mother and father time together after the children are in bed. The return to a new but manageable family life is reasonably complete.

—Brian Symon, M.D.

A Mom's Perspective:
Sleep Training Won't Just Happen on Its Own

You kind of just do this survival stuff as a parent for a while. There are certain things that fall into place naturally:

You don't have to teach them to eat. We offered food, and they ate it.

You don't force your kid to walk; they just do it.

You don't have to teach them to crawl; they're just going to do it.

Even now, our daughter amazes us with her ability to ride a scooter. I didn't teach her that. She just looked at it, watched other kids, and did it.

But I think sleep is one of the few things you really have to teach. You have to choose to do it. It's not just going to happen.

I know a lot of parents who agonize over their kids not yet sleeping through the night. But they're not doing anything to help them learn how. When I talk to my friends about this, I compare it to potty training: as parents, we have to create the environment and set some structure.

—Megan

2. Why Use Top-Up Bottles

This Is a Top-Up Bottle

The top-up bottle provides additional expressed breast milk (or formula) at night when the breasts have been drained but your baby is still hungry for more.

So, let's say that the 7:00 p.m. feeding is the last feeding of the day before you'd like your baby to go down for the night. You'll breastfeed your baby for the typical amount of time. At the very end, however, you'll seamlessly transition to offering a bottle. Your baby shouldn't even notice that the nipples have been switched. In some cases, she may not be actively 'asking' for more milk. While during daytime feeds you might easily take this state of contentment as a sign she is full, we encourage you to offer her more at this bedtime feed unless she is actively showing signs that she is full (e.g., turning away from the nipple).

At first, she may only take half an ounce of extra milk. But over time, she will start taking more and more top-up milk at this 7:00 p.m. feeding. These are the extra calories that will enable her to sleep much longer. With top-up bottles, your baby will more easily reach the first early milestone of going 3 hours between nighttime feedings.

Just as important, this is the beginning of getting your partner involved in the feedings. Top-up bottles, and later Dream Feed bottles, enable partners to contribute to feeding and sleep training. And, as we noted earlier, this is how you will get longer stretches of sleep.

You can use formula or expressed breast milk for a top-up bottle; it's entirely up to you and your pediatrician. To build up your expressed breast milk supply, take 15 more minutes at the end of a normal daytime feeding and pump any additional milk that you have. Your first 5–10 sessions probably won't produce much milk at all, but your body will gradually adjust. Soon you will be producing enough milk for a full breastfeeding plus an additional portion pumped for nighttime use.

You can start the first week, but you certainly don't have to. Start when you feel ready. Pumping from early on, in addition to your baby suckling on the breast, will trigger your body to produce more milk faster.

While pumping can start immediately, you won't immediately start using that expressed breast milk. Don't proceed with top-up bottles until your baby is successfully latching. For some mothers, successful breastfeeding will happen early and will be problem-free. Those mothers can move on to top-up bottles quite quickly. Other mothers will need more time to get to a consistent latch with their babies. In these cases, they should continue to persevere at breastfeeding until the baby is consistently feeding at the breast. As always, follow the specific advice from your pediatrician and lactation consultant over any general advice here.

Nipple confusion is not a concern with top-up bottles because of how and when they are introduced to your baby. By using top-up bottles only at night, in a very dark room, with a drowsy baby, there just won't be an opportunity to learn what a bottle looks like or remember what the sensation of sucking from an artificial nipple feels like. You'll find that your baby easily returns to the breast for all other feeds.

A Researcher's Perspective: Top-Up Bottles Can Be Really Helpful for the Baby and the Family

I have recommended early use of top-up bottles for many years. While it may seem a little counter intuitive, it is my experience that appropriate top-up bottles support and maintain breastfeeding. Improvement in breastfeeding success rates may be as high as 50%.

Using top-up bottles means that there can be a sharing of care. Many fathers enjoy the role of feeding one or two bottles per day. Grandmothers, of course, love helping out with a bottle-feed. Mothers who are tired have the chance for at least one block of extended sleep, which helps her milk supply for the next day.

Breast milk production varies from woman to woman and even from day to day. If it is your experience that you are unable to produce adequate volumes of expressed breast milk, that is just fine. Use formula. Or expressed breast milk. Remember that the key benefits to your child's immune system are established with even small volumes of your breast milk. These benefits are not diminished by the addition of formula or complementary feeding.

Almost all babies at some point will need a bottle of either expressed breast milk or formula—because mother's going on a trip or due to an unexpected event. If the baby has never before had a single bottle, this could pose a major problem. It can be traumatic for all involved if the baby refuses the bottle. Thus, I recommend that the baby have some bottle experience intermittently to keep the "skill" in place for those occasions when it is needed.

—Brian Symon, M.D.

Why Do We Care So Much About Top-Up Bottles?

At every stage of sleep training, your baby's sleep can only last as long as his belly still has milk in it. Once your baby is hungry, you may be able to hold him off for an extra 15 to 20 minutes, but you'll never make the kind of gains we want to go from a 3-hour to a 12-hour feeding (and sleep) cycle.

Your baby can handle more milk than you're providing in one breastfeeding session, and, with that extra milk, he will naturally sleep longer. To give him that milk, however, you have to provide a top-up bottle.

Additionally, almost all moms produce less milk at night than they do in the morning. This is an easily provable statement, but you will be stunned by how few people know it. We had a few moms who had to see for themselves, so they did their own experiment:

At 7:00 a.m., they pumped instead of breastfed. They measured how much they produced and then fed the milk by bottle back to their baby. That night at 7:00 p.m., they did the same thing. They all found that they produced, on average, half as much milk at the 7:00 p.m. feeding as they did during the 7:00 a.m. feeding.

There's just no way your baby is going to sleep for longer and longer periods at night if he's not starting with a full belly.

A Researcher's Perspective:
Your Milk Supply Lowers in the Evenings

I am very supportive of mothers who both breastfeed and bottle-feed. If you are using occasional bottles of expressed breast milk or formula to supplement your breastfeeding, you may find that the best outcomes occur when the bottles are given between 6:00 p.m. and midnight.

As almost all breastfeeding mothers have observed, there is better milk supply at 6:00 a.m. and a lower supply at 6:00 p.m. A mother's breast milk supply has a diurnal rhythm.

My rule of thumb is: "Trust a mother. Trust a baby." If it is your opinion that your baby is still hungry, then give yourself the freedom to give top-up formula or expressed breast milk. You know your baby better than any person; please trust your intuition.

I see many, many babies who are underweight, and, in a failed attempt to follow someone else's guidelines for exclusive breastfeeding, the baby's growth has been hindered. A hungry baby sleeps poorly. The baby who is overtired has a poorer appetite, and it all just swings out of control.

In addition to the clear benefits of making sure that the baby is fully fed, using appropriate top-up bottles gives a mother flexibility. Share the responsibility (and joy!) of feeding with your partner or a grandparent or a friend. Interestingly, by allowing a mother to have a little more rest and more flexibility, her breast milk supply improves and breastfeeding success increases.

—Brian Symon, M.D.

But What About Nipple Confusion?

If you mention your desire to introduce a bottle during the first month after birth, you will likely encounter some people who are very concerned about "nipple confusion." They will tell you that the introduction of a bottle in the first three months will cause your baby to reject the breast.

It will sound like nipple confusion is a raging pandemic afflicting millions of mothers everywhere. It will sound like avoiding bottles in the first three months demands as much discipline as keeping your baby away from cigarette smoke.

But there's no data backing up this fear. None. In fact, on the contrary: more and more doctors are now encouraging the introduction of a bottle before six weeks. As babies get older, there is a danger that they'll reject the bottle outright, limiting the flexibility of the mother as well as the involvement of the father.

**A Researcher's Perspective:
Supplemental Bottles Strengthen Lactation Success**

The concept of "nipple confusion" is perplexing to me. It's a term I never use and ask mothers not to use.

As a species, we are born with very few reflexes, but there are a few. One of those is sucking. Whether we place a little finger, mother's nipple, or a bottle's teat in the baby's mouth, a baby will suck. It's a reflex.

I have never seen a baby make a decision to move from breast to bottle simply because they have been given some complementary feeds. Babies almost always function logically.

In a situation where the breast milk supply is very low and bottles are available, the baby will make a decision and will show a preference for bottle-feeding. Where the mother has an adequate milk supply, babies are very content with a combined breast and bottle model of feeding. It is my very clear experience that a practice of combining breastfeeding with bottle supplementation supports, protects, and strengthens lactation and breastfeeding success.

—Brian Symon, M.D.

A Pediatrician's Perspective:
Nipple Confusion Is Pure Garbage

Babies who are nursing successfully are not going to be confused by a different nipple. Yes, we're absolutely pro-breastfeeding. But by the end of the first month at the very latest, you need to introduce a supplemental bottle so that dad or somebody else in the household can give the baby a bottle. Especially because many babies—if they've never seen an artificial nipple by six, seven, or eight weeks—will not take a bottle. They'll fight it. Even when they're hungry, they will hold out for nursing.

So, mothers who have to go back to work need to know that somebody else can give the baby food in their absence. If a couple wants to go out for dinner and somebody is going to watch the baby, a bottle is going to be necessary.

Don't worry about this hysteria over nipple confusion. The truth is quite the opposite. You want to introduce a bottle early on.

—Eileen Aicardi, M.D.

Nestlé and the World Health Organization

The hysteria over nipple confusion is overblown. To understand how it came to be, let's take a short historical tour and learn about the infamous Nestlé formula program.

In the 1970s, Nestlé and several other formula manufacturers decided to, in an act of self-described humanitarian aid, help impoverished mothers in developing countries feed their babies by providing free formula to hospitals.

When the program began, no one saw anything wrong with it. In developing countries, where doctors were concerned about the nutrition available to impoverished mothers, knowing for certain that babies were getting enough nutrients in the first two weeks was viewed very positively.

So, this program spread throughout the developing world. Nestlé, through relationships with hospitals, delivered millions and millions of dollars' worth of free formula. And the benefit to Nestlé was obvious—start these mothers on formula at the beginning, and they will buy more formula as their baby grows.

It took several years before health officials understood the implications of this decision. The rate of babies showing up malnourished increased dramatically. A malnourished baby in a developing country is not rare, so alarm bells didn't go off immediately. Also, because records weren't perfectly kept, it was hard to see that these malnourished babies were not isolated incidents, but part of a much larger trend. Finally, doctors realized what the malnourished babies shared in common: Nestle's free formula program.

Here's what had been happening:

Mothers who couldn't afford the formula after the first two weeks were still buying it, but were diluting it with water, not unlike what they had to do with all their foods. The babies were still getting formula, just not as rich. A year of overly diluted formula caused malnourishment in these newborns.

The malnourishment rates were dramatic compared to rates before the free formula program had started because providing free formula for the first two weeks compounded the problem.

In those first two weeks, mothers need their babies to suckle at the breast to stimulate milk production. That suckling action triggers the body to produce more milk. Because the mothers weren't breastfeeding during those critical first two weeks, their milk never came in.

When they left the hospital and their free formula ran out, they assumed they could go back to breastfeeding like they had for generations. But the breast milk just wasn't there; they had missed a critical window to communicate to their body to make milk. No matter what they tried, their milk supply never emerged. So, either they bought formula they couldn't afford and diluted it with water, or their babies went hungry on the breast. These mothers had no viable option.

Additionally, bottle-feeding caused new problems with which mothers in developing worlds never had to consider. Bottles have tiny parts that need to be washed and sanitized or else bacteria can grow inside them. The breast has bacteria as well, but the body is good at self-regulating it, and the bacteria passed from mother to baby is good bacteria. Bacteria that grows inside of an unsanitized nipple is not good bacteria. Doctors found that mothers were reusing the same bottle over and over again without any way to sanitize it. This resulted in malnourishment, infection, and disease spreading throughout newborns in the developing world.

At this point, the World Health Organization (WHO) got involved.

In 1981, faced with a malnourishment crisis in the developing world, coupled with spiking rates of infection, the WHO adopted Resolution WHA34.22, which banned the promotion of breast milk substitutes and gave health workers the responsibility to advise patients about the benefits and risks of breast milk versus formula.

In 1989, the WHO, jointly with UNICEF, issued a document called "Ten Steps to Successful Breastfeeding" and in 1990 published the "Innocenti

Declaration," which formally demanded that governments of the world adopt these 10 steps in all hospitals.

Every facility providing maternity services and care for newborn infants should:

1. Have a written breastfeeding policy that is routinely communicated to all healthcare staff.

2. Train all healthcare staff in skills necessary to implement this policy.

3. Inform all pregnant women about the benefits and management of breastfeeding.

4. Help mothers initiate breastfeeding within a half hour of birth.

5. Show mothers how to breastfeed, and how to maintain lactation even if they should be separated from their infants.

6. *Give newborn infants no food or drink other than breast milk, unless medically indicated.*

7. Practice rooming-in—allow mothers and infants to remain together—24 hours a day.

8. Encourage breastfeeding on demand.

9. Give no artificial teats or pacifiers (also called dummies or soothers) to breastfeeding infants.

10. Foster the establishment of breastfeeding support groups and refer mothers to them upon discharge from the hospital or clinic.

You'll notice number six deals with our subject at hand. Hospitals could no longer give bottles to babies.

By enforcing a strict rule across all hospitals, the WHO ensured that this practice of providing free formula to impoverished mothers would end and thus the generations-old tradition of breastfeeding would root itself once again.

This, plus an educational campaign about the benefits of breastfeeding, did in fact work, and most of the developing world returned to practices in place before Nestlé had intervened. Meanwhile, with a black eye that still hasn't healed, Nestlé pulled away from the marketing-to-the-developing-world game, as everywhere they went they faced organizations promoting boycotts of Nestlé.

A full 10 years after the WHO tried to resolve the Nestlé problem, several researchers began asking whether a strict bottle ban was necessary in all situations. For instance, would it be so wrong if the mother allowed the hospital to use a bottle the first night so that after a tough labor she could get a few hours of sleep? Would a single bottle cause nipple confusion and/or prevent the mother's milk from coming in? How about two bottles?

The WHO does not deal in small nuances like whether a few bottles here and there are okay. Their tool is a broad set of clear rules that can be implemented across hundreds of thousands of hospitals at once.

In 1997, Schubiger, Schwarz, and Tonz of the Neonatal Study Group in Lucerne, Switzerland, published a study in the *European Journal of Pediatrics* entitled "UNICEF/WHO Baby-Friendly Hospital Initiative: Does the Use of Bottles and Pacifiers in the Neonatal Nursery Prevent Successful Breastfeeding?" in which they concluded:

> In our study population, fluid supplements offered by bottle with or without the use of pacifiers during the first five days of life were not associated with a lower frequency or shorter duration of breastfeeding during the first six months of life.

After their work was published, most pediatricians in the developed world began to acknowledge that a few convenience bottles in the hospital would not cause problems.

A Researcher's Perspective: WHO Protocols Are Intended to Guide Developing Nations

I have spent years researching the WHO program on exclusive breastfeeding. It is important to understand the origins of the WHO protocols. They have an honorable ambition. That ambition is to decrease deaths from gastroenteritis in developing nations. These deaths are, to a very great extent, caused by contaminated water.

Fear of contaminated water is far less relevant in other parts of the world. If you live in a country with clean water and are competent at sterilizing bottle parts, these WHO protocols were never intended for you.

As a clinician, I am a strong supporter of breastfeeding. I am deeply concerned about these overly strict protocols for exclusive breastfeeding. Don't let protocols designed for a very different part of the world scare you or shame you against your own intuition.

—Brian Symon, M.D.

An Author's Perspective: Fed Is Best Is a Response to the WHO's Overly Stringent Guidelines

Where women used to claim that formula was excessively pushed on them, the preaching, both from many doctors and from fellow mothers, may now have gone too far the other way. Take the Baby-Friendly Hospital Initiative (BFHI). Established in 1991 by the WHO and UNICEF, the BFHI is an effort to help women around the world breastfeed exclusively from day one until a baby is 6 months old and for as long as possible once solid foods are introduced. It was meant to ensure proper nutrition, especially in regions that lack clean drinking water. But it has also been influential in the U.S. because it designates hospitals that conform to its rules as "baby-friendly."

If you walk into a BFHI-certified hospital, the signs will be clear: there are images everywhere of mothers nursing their babies. You won't see any formula, bottles, or pacifiers on display. Those are forbidden under BFHI guidelines, which state that human milk is "the normal way" to feed an infant. If a mother wants to formula-feed, this hospital must warn of "possible consequences" to the baby's health.

The pressure to room-in alarms some doctors. Last October, after several of Boston's largest hospitals shut down newborn nurseries to achieve the BFHI designation, three prominent physicians wrote a scathing viewpoint in *JAMA Pediatrics*, a leading peer-reviewed journal. "There is now emerging evidence that full compliance with the 10 steps of the initiative may inadvertently be promoting potentially hazardous practices and/or having counterproductive outcomes," wrote Dr. Joel L. Bass and Dr. Tina Gartley, both in pediatrics at Newton-Wellesley, and Dr. Ronald Kleinman, the physician-in-chief at MassGeneral Hospital for Children.

As Rachel Zaslow, a certified nurse-midwife in Charlottesville, Va., puts it, "The minute a person becomes pregnant, there's a notion that if you're not doing those kinds of things, you're not a good mother."

Last year, Dr. Christie Del Castillo-Hegyi, an emergency-room physician in Arkansas, founded Fed Is Best. The organization, run by a group of doctors, nurses, and mothers, raises awareness of feeding options. It wants the BFHI to reconsider its stringent rules and to inform mothers on what Del Castillo-Hegyi says are under-recognized risks of exclusive breastfeeding, ranging from jaundice to starvation. She would know. Several years ago, in her quest to exclusively breastfeed, she nearly starved her infant son to death. Some of the mothers who work with Fed Is Best have had similar experiences, in a few cases leading to their babies' death. They are determined to keep such tragedies from striking others. "If you have leaders telling you this is what's best, it becomes ideology, policy, identity," says Del Castillo-Hegyi. "I can't even think of something more vulnerable than motherhood. And if motherhood means '*exclusive breastfeeding*,' then a mother will do anything."

—Claire Howorth, *Time Magazine,* 2017, "The Goddess Myth: Motherhood Is Hard to Get Wrong. So Why Do So Many Moms Feel So Bad About Themselves?"

Nipple Confusion Confuses Everyone

In 1997, Marianne Neifert, Ruth Lawrence, and Joy Seacat from the Presbyterian/St. Luke's Medical Center in Denver, Colorado, and the Department of Pediatrics at the University of Rochester came out with a paper entitled "Nipple Confusion: Toward a Formal Definition."

This wasn't a study as much as a report that tried to provide the research community consistent language to describe what happens when a baby prefers a bottle to the breast.

There are no numbers in the paper. It's not a survey that shows the percentage of nipple confusion that happens in a larger population. There's no A/B test in this paper comparing a group of babies that received bottles versus those who didn't and then proving that nipple confusion occurs.

This is simply a paper that tried to provide a definition so that clinicians everywhere could use the same language.

Much to the surprise of the research community, but not surprising when you understand the backdrop of the fight with Nestlé, this language of nipple confusion quickly spread throughout the world as the newest danger smart mothers needed to avoid.

And even though the paper has no actual recommendation, and in fact was acknowledging that not enough research on the subject exists, pediatricians took this paper plus the WHO guidelines together and began recommending to every mother that she avoid bottles completely because of this newly defined fear of nipple confusion.

The actual lactation research community was fairly surprised by how quickly this spread in the nonscientific press. Chloe Fisher and Sally Inch of the John Radcliffe/Oxford Hospital, some of the leading lactation researchers in the world, wrote the following letter to the editor of *The Journal of Pediatrics* trying to calm the flames of this new fear:

> We would strongly question whether nipple confusion is a real entity. The normal term baby is born with a rooting reflex because feeding is a biologic imperative.

> In a neurologically and anatomically normal baby, turning the head in response to a touch of a cheek, opening the mouth wide, and putting the tongue down and forward (gaping) are reflex actions. With a deep mouthful of breast, the stimulus on the palate triggers sucking (rhythmic cycle of compression applied to the breast by the tongue).

> There is no evidence of which we are aware to support the view that the baby may forget how to do this if he is given something else to suck.

> Babies who have never been attached to the breast correctly, or who have been "manhandled" by unskilled helpers, may exhibit distress at the breast or "switch off" and refuse to feed. If this situation is "resolved" by giving a bottle, this pattern may be repeated on the next occasion and the baby will again refuse the breast. This baby has never been to the breast and is not confused; he is manifesting his distress. This may be interpreted by some as an apparent preference. If, however, the distressed baby has his hunger assuaged by some of his mother's milk (from a bottle), he may then be sufficiently calmed to allow a skilled caregiver to attach him to the breast correctly and gently.

In our practice, if the baby cannot be attached to the breast adequately or successfully by his mother, the priorities are that the mother produces milk (by expressing) and that the baby receives it (by bottle). This gives us and the mother time, and the baby can be offered the breast, with help, at each available opportunity, until he can do it himself. In no instance, in these circumstances, has a baby ever refused the breast, even when breast feedings have been separated by several days of exclusive bottle feeding.

We wonder if it is the grown-ups, rather than the babies, who are confused.

Five years later, in 2001, Donna Dowling and Warinee Thanattherakul of Case Western Reserve University published in their article, "Nipple Confusion, Alternative Feeding Methods, and Breast-Feeding Supplementation," their review of all the studies that had been done on nipple confusion since 1997. They conclude:

> The relationship between exposure to artificial nipples and pacifiers and the development of the aversive feeding behaviors associated with nipple confusion is neither refuted nor supported in the research literature. Despite this, recommendations given by health care providers to avoid bottle feeding continue to be driven by the belief in the phenomenon of nipple confusion.

Clearly, from this review of the literature it would be appropriate for health care providers to take a more moderate position when they educate parents.

For the most part, these conclusions have still not found the same popularity in the press that the original hysteria did.

Thus, for an entire generation of pediatricians and mothers, fear of nipple confusion has been commonplace when, in fact, there is really no scientific research anywhere that says nipple confusion is much of a problem for anyone.

A Researcher's Perspective: Limited Bottle Use Does Not Affect Breastfeeding Duration

A prospective study of breastfeeding mothers was undertaken to determine the effects of limited bottle use and infant temperament on breastfeeding outcomes. White, married, primigravida women who were committed prenatally to breastfeeding for at least six weeks (n = 121) were randomly assigned to one of two groups: a planned bottle group that would offer one bottle daily between the second and sixth week postpartum and a total breastfeeding group that would avoid bottles during the same period.

Group assignment had no effect on the occurrences of breastfeeding problems, on mothers' achievement of 90 percent of their prenatal breastfeeding duration goals, or on weeks to weaning across the study period.

Women, with support and motivation to breastfeed, have successfully combined breastfeeding and bottle supplements without unplanned weaning due to lack of milk.

We found no evidence that single daily bottle use in the early weeks postpartum is incompatible with prolonged breastfeeding among groups of women who are committed to breastfeeding.

Finally, no support was found for the nipple-confusion hypothesis.

—*Pediatrics,* 1992

A Pediatrician's Perspective: A Little Supplemental Formula Is Just Fine

Formula is not as good as breast milk, but it's pretty darn close. Formula in the fifties was a can of evaporated milk, one and a half cans of water, and two tablespoons of Karo syrup. That was formula. Talk about a sugar load. We've come a long way from there.

There are magic ingredients in breast milk that have yet to be recreated, this is true. So we always encourage mostly breast-feeding, if possible. But, on the other hand, to make a mom feel bad that she doesn't have enough milk or for whatever reason wants to supplement with formula, that's just not right.

—Eileen Aicardi, M.D.

A Mom's Perspective: Refusing the Bottle Is a Much Bigger Risk than Nipple Confusion

Our baby would cry for hours, like actual hours, with my partner holding her, stubbornly refusing to take the bottle. I had breast-fed exclusively for three months and then needed her to adapt to bottles before I went back to work. She just refused.

As a first-time mom, I wanted to follow every rule. I wish some-one had told me this could happen. I was so focused on breast-feeding correctly, I never even thought about bottle-feeding as well.

—Lauren (Mom of 2)

How to Make Bottle-Feeding Special

The truth is, for a mom who is breastfeeding, there really is nothing that replaces it. But the goal of top-up bottles is not to replace breastfeeding, it's just to supplement it. And bottle-feeding can still be an incredibly special time between a parent and the baby.

The key is preparation. You want everything you need for a top-up bottle to be ready to go before you start breastfeeding. As you finish feeding from the breast, you should be able to, in a single motion, remove the latch, insert the bottle, and continue the feeding. You'll still maintain skin-to-skin contact, and you'll allow your baby to continue the feeding uninterrupted.

For dads, the introduction of top-up bottles and nighttime replacement bottles presents a truly special opportunity. You get to share in this special moment of feeding your baby. If you're doing a top-up bottle, be positioned and ready to receive a seamless handoff of the baby in order to simulate an uninterrupted feed. Have your warm bottle ready and settle into the same dark, quiet environment in which the breastfeeding was occurring. Feel free to also have skin-to-skin contact. Just enjoy this quiet moment.

A Pediatrician's Perspective: Bottle Feeding Can Be a Time for Special Closeness

The term "nursing" means comforting and nourishing, whether by breast or bottle. Feeding time is more than just a time for nutrition. It is also a time for special closeness. The mutual giving that is part of breastfeeding should also be enjoyed during bottle-feeding. Besides giving your infant a bottle, give him your eyes, your skin, your voice, and your caresses. Baby will return to you more than just an empty bottle.

The special warmth of skin-to-skin contact can be accomplished by wearing short sleeves and partially undressing yourself and your baby when feeding. Hold the bottle alongside your breast as though it were coming from your body and look into your baby's eyes. Interact with your baby during a feeding. You want your baby to feel that the bottle is part of you. Most babies, breastfed and bottle-fed, feed better if you are quiet while they suck, but babies enjoy social interaction during pauses in the feedings. Watch your baby for signals that he wants to socialize during the feeding. Eventually you will develop an intuitive sense of your baby's feeding rhythm. Baby should feel that a person is feeding him, not just a bottle.

—Dr. William Sears, *The Baby Book*

3. Why Preempt Crying with Dream Feeds

This Is a Dream Feed

We are going to upend the most cherished and undisputed baby rule of all time. Yes, you can wake a sleeping baby. (Kind of.)

As the name suggests, a dream feed means feeding your baby without actually waking him up. This is how it will play out:

Your baby is still swaddled in his crib and sound asleep. Pick him up gently.

With either your breast or a warm bottle of expressed breast milk (or formula, your decision), ever so lightly, tickle his lips and cheek with the nipple.

While still asleep, he'll latch on and start sucking. It may take a few tries, but if he's hungry, he'll start feeding. Continue feeding and burping and feeding like normal. But don't make any effort to wake him up. Allow him to drift in and out of sleep, while his instinctual sucking motion takes over.

Put him back down.

He'll likely never truly wake up. This is a dream feed.

A Researcher's Perspective:
Dream Feeds Improve Sleep

Myth: Never wake a sleeping baby.
Fact: Waking her up for an 11:00 p.m. dream feed (an extra couple of ounces) may be the key step in improving her sleep.

—Harvey Karp, M.D., *The Happiest Baby Guide to Great Sleep*

Use Dream Feeds to Preempt Crying

This is the most common routine that almost all new parents face several times a night. We call it cry-and-respond. Your baby goes through a roller coaster of sleep, agitation, and then struggles to sleep again. Rinse and repeat minutes later.

sleep —> wake —> cry —> feed —> burp —> change
—> re-swaddle —> soothe —> sleep

Your baby is asleep. And then she wakes up. And then she starts crying, which wakes you up.

You frantically grab your baby before her crying gets too agitated.

Then she feeds.

After feeding her, you burp her, change her, and re-swaddle her. All of which wakes her up...

So, you'll start the entire soothing process again, hoping and praying that she'll find her way back to sleep. But because she's so awake and you're so tired, it feels that much more challenging. In many cases, it actually is.

This is a long process, and it's a lot of awake time for both you and your baby. When you want your baby to learn how to sleep at night, she's going through this pretty intense process of waking up, crying, feeding, being changed, being re-swaddled...all the while: awake.

And then the baby's just expected to soothe herself back to sleep? That's a tall order.

There's a bookshelf of books on how to teach self-soothing, but the reality is that for most babies, it's too hard to do and most parents realize that pretty quickly. We have a section in this book on low-stimulation soothing, but we all know that concept goes right out the window if your baby is wailing. Low-stimulation soothing only works when your baby is *slightly* agitated, but it doesn't work when she's off-the-charts wailing.

So, here is the absolute magic of the Dream Feed Method.

We're going to take this unfortunate, painful, borderline tortuous routine that parents know all too well:

sleep —> wake —> cry —> feed —> burp —> change
—> re-swaddle —> soothe —> sleep

And we're going to replace it with this much simpler, much quicker routine:

sleep —> dream feed —> sleep

You preempted the nighttime awakening. Your baby never became agitated. His belly gets re-filled. And he barely even noticed.

A Researcher's Perspective: Think of It Like Topping Off the Gas Tank on Your Car

If your baby wakes up hungry each night, in addition to boosting her daytime milk, it makes sense to boost her evening calories. (Think of it like topping off the gas tank on your car by filling it to the brim.)

A dream feed is when you wake a sleeping baby to give her an extra feed.

Dream feeds are great for your infant because:

- She'll get the extra calories she needs to sleep better.

- The meal is at a convenient time (so you sleep longer).

- The feeding is not in response to her crying (which would only reward the waking and end up encouraging more night feeding!).

The idea is to wake her before she wakes you so you're giving her the nourishment she needs, but not rewarding her for waking and crying.

—Harvey Karp, M.D., *The Happiest Baby Guide to Great Sleep*

Why Have I Never Heard of Dream Feeds?

Dream Feed is not a new term we invented. The late Tracy Hogg and her co-author Melinda Blau created the term in 2000 in *Secrets of the Baby Whisperer*:

Tank them up. This might sound like a rather crude expression, but one of the ways we get babies to sleep through the night is by filling their tummies. To that end, when an infant is six weeks old, I suggest two practices: cluster feeding—that is, feed her every 2 hours before bedtime—and giving what I call a dream feed right before you retire for bed. For example, you give her the breast (or a bottle) at six and eight in the evening, and the dream feed at ten-thirty or eleven. With dream feeding, literally nurse or bottle-feed her in her sleep. In other words, you pick your baby up, gently place the bottle or breast on her lower lip, and allow her to eat, taking care not to wake her. When she's finished, you don't even burp her; just put her down. Infants are usually so relaxed at these feeds, they don't gulp air. You don't talk; you don't change her unless she's soaked through or soiled. With both these tanking-up techniques, most babies can sleep through that middle-of-the-night feed, because they have enough calories to keep them going for 5 or 6 hours. Tip: Have Dad take over the dream feed. Most men are usually home at that time, and most love doing it.

Many parents start doing a dream feed around the fourth month, because they hear about it from a friend or read *Secrets of the Baby Whisperer*. They fall in love with it immediately because of how easy it is.

But before that fourth month, many parents don't even consider it for a few reasons.

First, many parents don't know that a baby's sucking action is physically instinctual, even while still asleep. When you touch a nipple (whether from a breast or a bottle) to a hungry baby's lips, she will start sucking on it even when fast asleep. When you see it for the first time, it's surprising to watch. But once you start doing it regularly, you will never want to go back.

Many parents also don't know that the dream feed is much easier to do with a bottle than the breast. Because the milk comes easily from a bottle, a sleeping baby that starts instinctually sucking will receive milk immediately without struggling through the let-down process that is a regular part of feeding from the breast. It also helps that when feeding with a bottle, you can hold a baby upright instead of on her side. It is possible to do a dream feed from the breast, but the quantity of milk that the baby will take is sometimes much less than from a bottle. And every mom has experienced the baby falling asleep on her breast. With a bottle-based dream feed, it's easier to keep the baby sucking. Our suggestion is to at least try both and do what works for you.

Many parents assume diaper changes must happen with every feeding. Modern-day disposable diapers are incredible at wicking moisture away and holding it inside the diaper but removed from your baby's skin. A combination of a wicking diaper plus a petroleum-based ointment means that your baby can lie there with a wet diaper for much longer than 3 hours. The proof of this is easily observable. If you try it, and your baby's skin continues remains rash-free, then it's fine to continue doing it. And if you skip diaper changing during the night and see that your baby's delicate tushy is starting to look red, then you need to change more often.

Some parents don't try a dream feed before the fourth month because they're taking self-soothing advice too far. Because the crying-it-out method has dominated the sleep-training conversation for the last 35 years, many parents assume that every sleep-training situation requires some period where the baby needs to cry. If you do the Dream Feed Method and start early, self-soothing is not nearly as important. While self-soothing is the dominant piece of most sleep-training ideologies, for the Dream Feed Method it's just not the most important step.

While you won't find the words *dream feed* in any peer-reviewed research, you'll find quite a few mentions of "focal feedings" in the literature, which is effectively the same thing. And the research has shown repeatedly that teaching parents to offer what they call focal feeds in the first few months has statistically significant outcomes in randomly controlled trials.

A Researcher's Perspective: Dream Feeds Promote Longer Sleep with No Effect on 24-Hour Milk Intake

The study objective was to investigate whether exclusively breastfed infants could be taught to sleep through the night (defined from 12:00 a.m. to 5:00 a.m.) during the first eight weeks of life. Treatment parents were instructed to offer a focal feed (between 10:00 p.m. and midnight) to their infants every night to gradually lengthen intervals between middle-of-the-night feeds.

By three weeks, treatment infants showed significantly longer sleep episodes at night. By eight weeks 100 percent of treatment infants were sleeping through the night compared to 23 percent of control infants.

Treatment infants were feeding less frequently at night but compensated for the relatively long nighttime interval without a feed by consuming more milk in the early morning. Milk intake for the 24-hour periods did not differ between groups.

It concluded that parents can have a powerful influence on the development of their infants' sleep patterns.

—Teresa Pinilla and Leann Birch, *Pediatrics*, February 1993, "Help Me Make It through the Night: Behavioral Entrainment of Breast-Fed Infants' Sleep Patterns"

No More Cry-and-Respond

Once you start doing dream feeds instead of the standard cry-and-respond routine, you'll find that several other major parenting questions are easier to answer.

First, you'll no longer have to co-sleep if you don't want to. While we acknowledge that a lot of people believe in co-sleeping philosophically, there are some who would have preferred not to co-sleep but ended up doing it out of necessity. Having your baby right near you shortens the time from when your baby wakes up agitated and you start feeding. The pure convenience of pulling your crying baby immediately to the breast is what makes co-sleeping so appealing.

But co-sleeping brings some challenging implications to sleep training because it encourages frequent snacking instead of full meals. It also creates an association of a baby sleeping near her mother, which, when you eventually break that habit later on, will lead to a loss of familiarity. Many mothers are then regrettably forced into a cry-it-out or sleepless nights decision. Dream feeds remove this need because you're not actually waiting to hear your baby cry in the middle of night. You set your alarm for your predetermined feeding period, and you get up and feed your baby. There's no frantic rushing around.

Second, cry-and-respond excludes your spouse from bottle-feeding. It's really hard for him to help in the middle of the night if you wait for your baby to start crying because of how agitated the baby will become during the wait for a warmed bottle. In those 3 or 4 minutes of preparing the bottle, a fussy baby turns into a wailing one, which leaves a tough choice for the parents. Most couples eventually just stop relying on the dad in the middle of the night.

And finally, cry-and-respond can unfortunately lead to cry-it-out. Once you start a routine of soothing your baby after this extended feeding process, your baby becomes reliant upon your soothing. And then when you finally decide that you've had enough of late nights and just can't handle it anymore, you have to wean your baby off of that soothing—by crying-it-out.

An Author's Perspective: Promote Quiet Nighttime Feedings

If you let her get to the point where arms are flying and mouth is screaming, it will be harder for her to fall asleep again after she is done eating. Remember, these nighttime feedings should enable your baby to go right back into a deep, restful sleep.

—Suzy Giordano "The Baby Coach," *Twelve Hours' Sleep by Twelve Weeks Old*

4. Why Dream Feed a Little Bit Earlier Each Night

The Challenge with Stretching-It-Forward

Stretching forward is the default technique every other sleep-training book recommends. In this method, you let your baby sleep as long as she can, and then you try to get her to go a few minutes longer each night. Most parents can successfully drop one of the feedings by the second or third month. Their schedule can often look something like this:

Figure 1. Stretching-Forward Method Schedule

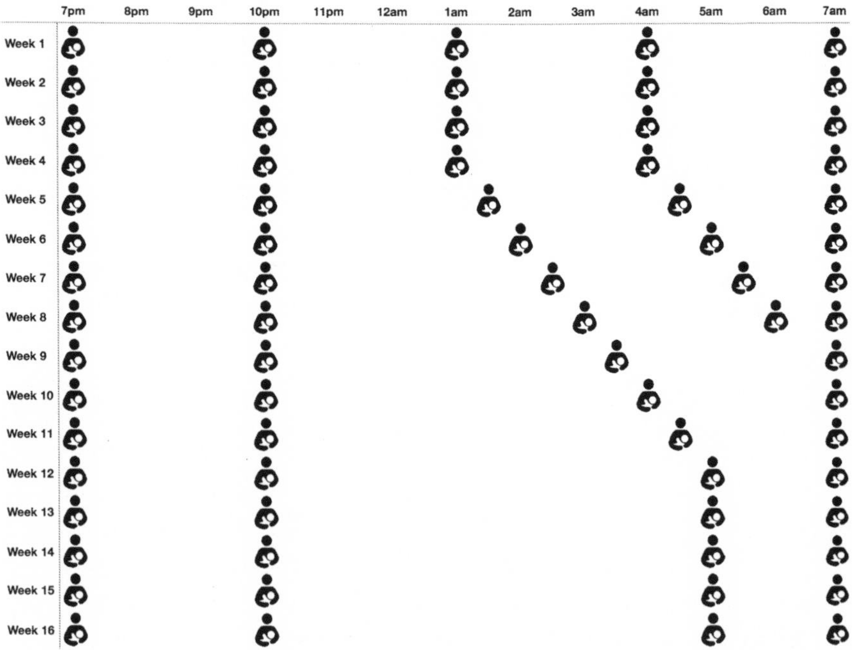

This itself does not seem like bad progress. And most parents that drop one or two feedings in the first four months and are down to just a 10:00 p.m. feeding and/or a 4:00 a.m. or 5:00 a.m. feel pretty good about the progress.

But the problem is that a lot of them get stuck there. It gets increasingly difficult to get rid of that 4:00 a.m. feeding.

It's the middle of the night. Mom is exhausted. Dad is exhausted. All they want is for their baby to stop crying and go back to sleep. But some book they read told them to help their baby stretch forward a little bit longer.

They are left with some form of 4:00 a.m. to 5:00 a.m. wakeup that becomes, frankly, intractable. It proves impossible to get a baby to stretch out those last few hours when you're trying to do it in the middle of the night.

This pattern for many babies will continue for months. Or years. Seriously, years. And either you just accept it, or you break down and do cry-it-out. No parent *wants* to do cry-it-out. But for most, there comes a time when they just simply can't take the lack of sleep anymore.

Instead, Dream Feed a Little Earlier Each Night

With the Dream Feed Method, you simply feed your baby a little bit *earlier* each night. For many, this might sound counter-intuitive, but stick with us. What follows is an overview of how dream feeds turn 3-hour sleep durations into a single 12-hour sleep duration.

The foundation is getting to consistent, predictable 3-hour sleep durations, measured from the beginning of one feeding to the beginning of the next. Let's say you're there. Your baby comfortably starts her feedings at 7:00 p.m., 10:00 p.m., 1:00 a.m., 4:00 a.m., and 7:00 a.m. (Your actual schedule can start whenever you like, but we'll talk about 7:00 p.m. to 7:00 a.m. for consistency.) You start this phase of the Dream Feed Method when your baby can achieve these 3-hour stretches between nighttime feedings without significant intervention from the parents. For many parents, the sweet spot occurs in the middle of the second month.

You're going to lock in 7:00 a.m. as the first feeding of the day and not move it throughout this whole process, and you're going to move the 4:00 a.m. feeding earlier at small intervals.

Your first step is to move that 4:00 a.m. feeding back to 3:45 a.m., preempting your baby's wake-up with a dream feed. Now your baby has a full belly, is resting quietly, is still swaddled tightly, and is ready to continue sleeping. You already know your baby is accustomed to going 3 hours until the 7:00 a.m. feeding. By moving his dream feed back by 15 minutes, you will find on the first morning that he wakes up exactly 3 hours later at 6:45 a.m.

Now you will need to hold him off from feeding until 7:00 a.m. You can rock him, sing to him, or bounce him. You can use a pacifier or a vibrating swing. One mom we know would stand by the open kitchen window, enjoying some fresh air while her son alternated between whimpers and contentment. Ignore everything you've ever read about self-soothing during these 15 minutes. You just have to hold him off for 15 minutes—without feeding him. If this feels uncomfortable to you, we understand. It's hard to feel as if you're denying your baby what he wants. This can be a great opportunity to call in a reinforcement...Dads have the added advantage of *not* smelling of breast milk. A little distance from the food source can help babies feel a little more patient during these waiting periods.

Your baby will adjust quickly. When you successfully reach 7:00 a.m. three days in a row without too much struggle, the ratchet is set. Your baby has now proven he can go from 3:45 a.m. to 7:00 a.m. You've lengthened that last sleep period to 3 hours and 15 minutes. Congratulations, you've started sleep training.

You're going to keep stretching earlier throughout the night:

Figure 2. Dream Feed Ratcheting-Back Method Schedule

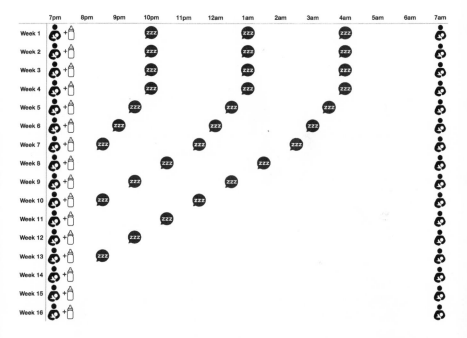

A few observations about this schedule.

Notice how after week eight, you never need to feed your baby from 2:00 a.m. to 7:00 a.m. For millions of parents, waking up between 2:00 a.m. and 7:00 a.m. is a way of life. You won't have that burden because your baby is never going to become accustomed to that early wakeup.

Now, notice how easy the last four to eight weeks are. The final "middle of the night" feedings in those weeks all occur before 11 p.m. Either you or your partner can just stay up for that feeding and then go to sleep for the rest of the night. For many parents, the exhausting part is done at this point!

That's why the Dream Feed Method is such an important technique.

First, it's a thousand times easier to do than stretching forward. Instead of trying to help your baby sleep from 3:00 a.m. to 4:00 a.m. to 5:00 a.m. to 6:00 a.m., enduring the tortures of hearing her cry in the middle of the night, you'll be working in the other direction. Your most challenging period of holding her off will consistently occur between 6:45 a.m. and 7:00 a.m., when at least one of you is up for the day, rested, and ready to soothe your baby. Sounds much easier, right?

The incredible benefit is much more long lasting. Your baby won't ever become accustomed to waking at 5:00 a.m. Your toddler won't wake up at 5:00 a.m. Your preschooler won't wake up at 5:00 a.m.

And you won't wake up at 5:00 a.m.

A Dad's Perspective: My Friends Were Baffled by All of This

I can't tell you how many people were baffled by our dedication to stretching the 4:00 a.m. feeding backwards—especially when our baby dropped all of the other feedings on his own. So by two and a half months, we were only doing the 4:00 a.m. feeding, and we dutifully stretched it backwards by 15 minutes for a month and a half.

Honestly, it meant that we never had to hold him off at night, he never cried, and it made the payoff of 12 hours of sleep that much sweeter when we weren't worried about the dreaded 4:00 a.m. feeding—because that feeding is the absolute worst. It's way too close to morning so you and baby have difficulty going back to sleep afterwards!

—Stephen (Dad of two)

All Sleep Training Methods Involve Holding Off

Every method out there, from the Dream Feed Method to Cry-It-Out to Baby Wise, is a variation on how to hold your baby off, either from needing additional soothing in the middle of the night or from needing to feed in the middle of the night. The end of sleep training is when your baby sleeps without your intervention.

One of the things you'll learn by doing the Dream Feed Method is that it doesn't actually matter if you hold your baby off from other types of soothing as long as the period between feedings is slowly stretching out. When you offer a dream feed 15 minutes earlier than the previous night, say 2:15 a.m. instead of 2:30 a.m., and your baby wakes up 15 minutes earlier the next morning, say 6:45 a.m. instead of 7:00 a.m., it's okay to rush into the nursery before your baby is wailing and soothe her. You're just holding her off from feeding at 6:45 a.m.

She'll be soothable for those 15 minutes, even if it takes a little extra effort. Shushing and bouncing and singing and pacifiers. That small period of being held off from feeding teaches her that she can do it again. Your baby, the next night, will learn to take a slightly bigger feeding knowing that she needs to go slightly longer. The next night she'll learn not to be so upset when her belly is 80 percent empty, because just a few minutes away is another feeding that will fill it up.

These small periods of holding her off, which, when done right, only last for 10 to 15 minutes, stretch out her expectation of how often she'll feed. While the Dream Feed Method might initially feel complicated because you have to diligently think through when each feeding will occur, in reality, your baby is leading the way. She's telling you whether she's ready for a longer stretch, and thus an earlier dream feed, by making it to 7:00 a.m. easily. She may still wake up before then. She may even need some soothing as she gets more accustomed to being awake in her own bed. But she's ready when getting to 7:00 a.m. feels easy. And don't worry, later on in the step-by-step instructions, we'll talk about what to do if it ever doesn't feel easy.

The first few weeks can be tough. You may be filled with some uncertainty, because no baby is 100 percent consistent—far from it. But once you start making progress, you're going to see that success is possible. Perhaps for the first time, you'll start to believe what we've been saying all along: that yes indeed, you can do this.

Cry-It-Out: Effective But Sooooooo Unpleasant

Now let's talk about the most popular (infamous?) alternative to the Dream Feed Method. While there are many names and variations of the cry-it-out method, from the *extinction method* to the *graduated extinction method* to the *progressive interval approach*, they all are largely the same. They begin in the fourth month or beyond and entail weaning your baby off of soothing by allowing her to cry for longer and longer periods of time.

Whatever the variation, the cry-it-out method works, but it's an awful lot of unpleasantness to endure—for both you and your baby.

The efficacy of the method has been validated in dozens of peer reviewed, randomly controlled studies. Except in a small percentage of actual sleep disorders, the cry-it-out method almost always works in transitioning babies from getting up multiple times a night to settling down to what researchers refer to as "through the night," which means sleeping uninterrupted from midnight to 5:00 a.m. The crying-it-out process generally takes several nights depending on how aggressively the parents employ it. And it generally always involves many hours of straight crying. Whether you believe prolonged crying causes long-term harm to your baby is a subject debated extensively. What is undeniable, however, is that many parents would choose to avoid it if they could. Even the most motivated parents will find that crying-it-out is one of the most emotionally challenging experiences as a new parent. Every instinct in your body will tell you that this is wrong. The heartbreak and anguish of every hour of wailing that goes by is unreal.

The cry-it-out method also features repeated regressions, so it's not a one-and-done process. Many parents report having to repeat the experience many times over the course of their baby's first few years.

Additionally, because so many parents are nervous about doing the cry-it-out method, they wait longer to do it, which not only makes it worse but also extends the time that they're getting up multiple times a night. The range of periods for trying the cry-it-out method for the first time is anywhere from the fourth month all the way into the twelfth month and beyond, extending the period of sleeplessness that both baby and parent have to endure.

The Dream Feed Method Just Feels Better

The beauty of the Dream Feed Method is not only that it works in helping your baby learn how to sleep from dusk till dawn, but that it also does so with the least amount of pain endured by both the parents and the baby. Here's why:

Middle-of-the-night wake-ups end two-thirds of the way through the process because the Dream Feed Method stretches backwards. The last remaining feeding to drop at the end of the process is not the 4:00 a.m. or 5:00 a.m. feeding; it's the 9:00 p.m. or 10:00 p.m. feeding. This means your last month of finishing the sleep training process will be actually quite easy!

Because the Dream Feed Method utilizes supplemental bottles, both parents are able to share nighttime feeding responsibilities. By the third week, you could already be switching off feedings with your partner and sleeping 6 hours in a row. By the eighth week, you could alternate nights with your partner and take off every other night completely.

The Dream Feed Method doesn't rely on crying to teach self-soothing as its primary form of adjusting your baby's sleep patterns. There is never a time where you have to listen to your baby cry for hours, wondering whether short- or long-term harm is being done.

The Dream Feed Method preempts crying at night, so you don't have to wake up with a start as your baby wakes you, wakes your partner, and wakes anyone else in the house while you sprint around trying to settle her down. You set an alarm clock, wake up fifteen minutes before she is likely to need a feeding, and provide her the feeding right before she would've needed it. It's a fast and peaceful process that everyone else in your household will sleep right through.

And finally, the Dream Feed Method works. The nighttime feedings will disappear. Your baby will sleep from dusk till dawn.

And Yes, You Can Also Just Do Stretch-It-Forward

As we have stated throughout the book, there is no one-size-fits-all approach, and you are empowered to pick and choose the parts of the Dream Feed Method that work for you.

We have seen a lot of success using dream feeds to prevent crying and shifting feedings earlier each night instead of asking the baby to stretch further. But it can absolutely work to stretch forward as well. So, let's spend a few minutes talking about how to get past the most common pitfalls with stretching-it-forward.

As we discussed earlier, the two problems with stretching-it-forward are that the hard work of holding off is done in the middle of the night around that 4:00 a.m. feeding and that parents inevitably become too exhausted to keep trying. This ultimately leaves them stuck with a consistent 4:00 a.m. feeding.

Step 1: Provide a great 11:00 p.m. feeding with a top-up bottle

If you've already removed the 10:00 p.m. or 11:00 p.m. feeding, it may feel counterintuitive to reintroduce it but that's exactly what we're recommending. The reality is that it will be easier to get rid of that 11:00 p.m. feeding later than it will be to stretch-it-forward from 4:00 a.m. to 7:00 a.m. when the last feeding is at 7:00 p.m. That's simply too long a span for your baby to make until later in this sleep training process. So, if you've already gotten rid of the 11:00 p.m. feeding, reintroduce it.

If you currently have a 10:00 p.m. feeding, try to stretch-it-forward to 11:00 p.m. You don't need to fight it. If your baby is making it to 10:00 p.m. and 11:00 p.m. isn't going to happen easily, then you can do the following steps with a 10:00 p.m. feeding. However, if there's a chance you can let that feeding drift closer to 11:00 p.m., it will make the later stages of the morning a bit easier.

The most important step here is to make this 11:00 p.m. a great feeding. Provide a full regular feeding either by breast or by bottle, and make sure your baby's belly is full with a top-up bottle.

Step 2: Wake up in anticipation of the next feeding

Next, you want to allow your baby to prove to herself and to you how long she can sleep. You're going to let her lead the way. If she's been sleeping until 4:00 a.m. and then waking up for a feeding, you wait for her to make it past 4:00 a.m. naturally. Soon she should give you a night where she lasts until 4:15 a.m.

The next night you need to still get up at 4:00 a.m. in case she wakes up early. At 4:00 a.m., you're up and ready to go. You have your warm bottle ready if this is a bottle feed. You're in the room or watching on the monitor.

Your goal is to help your baby make it to 4:15 a.m. again just like she did the night before. And if she wakes up early, you're prepared to hold her off without her getting overly agitated.

This is the trick of stretching-it-forward. You still get up preemptively to keep your baby calm, as she gets closer to waking up. So, for night number two, you get up at 4:00 a.m. and your baby only makes it to 4:10 a.m. this time. Now you have five minutes of holding off to do. By being there and ready to go, you can gently soothe her while she's still lying down. You can rock her, bounce her, or sing to her. Anything you want to get that last five minutes. Once you reach 4:15 a.m., you're ready to go with a feeding either at the breast or by a bottle.

If you skip this little step of waking up preemptively, your baby wakes up alone, crying for more food. By the time you get there, she's going to be wailing. There's just no chance with your baby wailing at 4:10 a.m. that you're going to hold her off for five minutes. It's just too much to ask, especially if you're going to do it for weeks. The whole key is keeping them calm during the night, so you don't have to spend so much time soothing them back to a calm state.

Step 3: Keep ratcheting forward by ~10 minutes per night

Once your baby is consistently getting to 4:15 a.m., you start setting your alarm later as well. You're trying to make on average ten minutes of progress a night, or about an hour a week. If you're starting this process with your baby waking up at 4:00 a.m., plan on it taking you three weeks to get to 7:00 a.m. That's three weeks of one parent per night setting an alarm and waking up a few minutes before your baby wakes up.

Stretching-it-forward can absolutely work. We don't think it works faster or slower than the Dream Feed method, but it does take dedication.

Those last couple hours in the morning can be really tough, and it hits you when you're already significantly sleep deprived. This means you really need to spend some time thinking about how you're going to make it a consistent routine. Which partner is getting up? Is it a reasonable expectation that they're going to get up each morning ahead of the baby crying?

The teamwork piece is important here. Ideally, you want whoever is doing the hard work at 4:00 a.m. to be responsible for as little as possible with the preceding feeding. Your best chance for success is your partner goes to sleep as early as possible, wakes up at 4:00 a.m. reasonably refreshed and ready to put in the work necessary to soothe your baby until feeding time.

You have to pick the right pattern for you and your family dynamic. Our unscientific observation has been that it works a little bit better if you switch off with the 4:00 a.m. responsibilities. It's certainly doable for one person to get it done, but switching off means that whoever is responsible that night has just had a full night's sleep, and you run a smaller risk of getting fatigued from this too early.

Another nice component of switching off is you get into a nice rhythm of feeling like you owe it to your partner. If mom can successfully get the baby to 4:30 a.m. on one night, then dad knows he needs to be able to do the same the next night. You'll start rooting for each other—even waking up excited to hear how far your baby made it the night before.

Step 4: Remove the 11:00 p.m. feeding

Once you successfully move the 4:00 a.m. feeding to 7:00 a.m., you have several options to remove the 11:00 p.m. feeding. You can stretch it backwards using preemptive Dream Feeds or you can reduce the quantity over time. Nothing changes here compared to how it was described earlier.

If after reading this section, the stretch-if-forward process sounds more intuitive to you than the backward stretching model that we described earlier, just go for what feels right to you. If you start making small but consistent ten-minute extensions, that's proof alone that it's working. If you successfully shift your baby from waking up at 4:00 a.m. to 5:00 a.m. and you've proven to yourselves that the process that made this happen was deliberate and not just an accident, then there's a very high likelihood that you will make it all the way from 5:00 p.m. to 7:00 a.m.

As always, pick what's right for you, and give it your best shot. You can do this.

Figure 3. Stretch-It-Forward General Schedule:

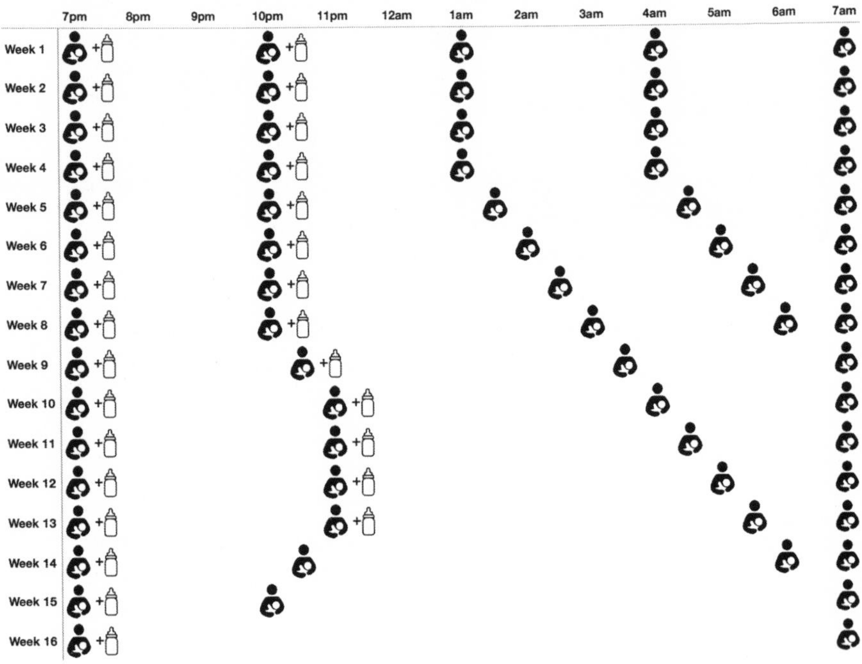

Feeding plus a Top-Up Bottle

Normal feeding when baby awakes (breast and/or bottle)

Dream Feed (breast and/or bottle)

A Dad's Perspective: Sometimes You Get a Big Jump in One Night

I still remember one morning when I got up with my alarm at 4:45 a.m. and, in a daze, sat at the kitchen table with the baby monitor, waiting for our son to wake up. I was still planning on going back to sleep afterwards, so I was kind of disappointed when he didn't wake up for his scheduled 5:00 a.m. feeding, which is how far he made it to the night before. At 5:15 a.m. I was actually a little annoyed, because I saw my opportunity to go back to sleep dwindling. There he was sleeping peacefully. A whimper here and a whimper there, but clearly not yet awake.

At 5:30, I finally made some coffee and ate some breakfast. At this point, I'd already heated the bottle three times, thinking that the feeding would surely be imminent. And yet still he slept soundly. Finally, at 6:00 a.m., he woke up and I went in and fed him with just a little two-ounce bottle to hold him off for the hour before his 7:00 a.m.

It really felt like magic. I couldn't wait for my wife to wake up and hear that he'd had made it all the way to 6:00 a.m. I was a wreck at work that day, but I still remember how proud I felt of our little guy, and how relieved my wife and I were knowing that the hard work of sleep training was just about over. Once he got to 6:00 a.m., it only took a few more nights for him to get all the way to 7:00 a.m., and he's never gone back.

—Will (Dad of one)

PART 3:

The Dream Feed Method Step-By-Step

"Having children is like living in a frat house—
Nobody sleeps, everything's broken,
and there's a lot of throwing up."

—Ray Romano

1. Start in the First Four Months: Weeks One Through Four

Goals:

✓ **Recover from delivery**

✓ **Establish good breastfeeding**

✓ **Start pumping and storing breast milk**

Recovering at the Hospital

First off, congratulations! For those of you having your first child, an extra big congratulations!

If there were any complications with the baby, then the doctors are in charge right now. If your baby was premature or had a difficult delivery or needs some extra care and attention, then your doctors and nurses are going to take over, and you'll just do whatever you are instructed to do.

From a Dream Feed Method perspective, there's obviously nothing you need to think about. You can make no wrong decisions. Don't worry about scheduled feedings or on-demand. Don't worry about anything related to sleep training. Recover. Enjoy your baby.

When you're ready, we'll be here.

Helping Mom Sleep at the Hospital

Being at the hospital has many pros and one big con. The pros are that you have a team of professionals who are there for you and your baby. Your nurses are an early warning system in case something's not right. They do a ton of teaching. You'll learn about caring for your baby, breastfeeding, burping, swaddling, and everything else that you might not remember from the class you took three months prior, when nothing seemed real.

One major con is that it's nearly impossible to sleep at the hospital. To understand why, you have to consider how the hospital functions. The maternity ward at a hospital is like a shopping mall filled with different stores. Instead of you going into each store, each store sends a representative to you. The list is endless. Your obstetrician, the pediatrician, a new nurse every 12 hours, a lactation consultant, the birth certificate, a hearing test, social security, the hospital photographer, and more. Each of these people has a dozen rooms or more to get to during each shift. That's called making their rounds. It's nearly impossible to coordinate all of those people; so instead, they show up whenever you're next on their list, whether you're trying to sleep or not. You may have been up for 48 straight hours, but there will be a knock at your door every 20 minutes with somebody trying to check you off his or her list. And, this is before we even start talking about friends and family members wanting to visit.

Here's our biggest piece of advice for getting a little more sleep at the hospital, the time in which you need it most. Pick the times you're going to sleep. Tell your nurse and put a sign on the door. The nurses are used to this request, but will only do it if you ask. You'll have a little sign that says, "Please don't knock on the door. Mother is sleeping. Talk to nurses' station first," and all these various people doing their rounds will have to come to the nurse and ask. Additionally, the nurse will now try to stack up as many tasks as possible both before and after your sleep period. Doing something like this does make it a little bit harder on everyone who is just trying to do his or her job, but truthfully it's a small inconvenience and they all also want you to sleep.

A reasonable request is to talk to the nurse once you catch your breath after being transported from the delivery room to your two-day room on the maternity ward. Ask for three 3-hour blocks per day where you can be guaranteed of no interruptions. Two of those will be at night and one of them can be either in the mid-morning or mid-afternoon. You can then also coordinate your social visits so that friends and family avoid visiting during these times.

Now after probably the longest period of time you've ever spent awake, you'll be positioned to claim a few hours of deep, uninterrupted sleep.

While we're discussing the subject of mom's rest in the hospital, we'll throw in our two cents on using the hospital nursery. Similar to how we'll address the subject of breastfeeding, we believe a baby near its mother is best. We also believe a mother's rest is pretty important. And sometimes these two beliefs conflict.

Our advice: absolutely feel free to use that nursery for one, two, or three of these sleep periods. It's quite literally the best trained, highest priced babysitters you'll ever hire.

Partners, ensuring mom gets some sleep is fundamentally your job. You'll be tired, too, so you should sleep when she sleeps, but it's on you to make all this happen. No one will want to mess with a partner standing guard over sleeping mama bear.

A Mom's Perspective: First Night in the Hospital

We had been up for 36 hours. My labor started at 9:00 p.m., so we had been that entire day and then we were up all the next day. That night, the baby actually slept surprisingly well. I remember waking up feeling worried that he wasn't breathing. (How else could he be so quiet?) But the next night was the total opposite. He just would not sleep in his bassinet in the hospital room. I would feed him, and he'd fall asleep, and then I would quietly congratulate myself: *I'm such an awesome mom. Look at me with my sleeping newborn. Let me put him back in his bassinet.* And then he would wake after about three minutes.

It was three in the morning. I finally had had enough. I desperately needed to get some sleep, David was sleeping in the chair, and I had this fear of falling asleep with Oliver in my arms and then dropping him over the edge of the hospital bed. I finally gave in and rang for the nurse, who promptly took Oliver to the nursery.

The moment that they took him away, I just completely lost it. I was hysterically crying and spouting something about being the worst mother in the world, while David tried to calm me down. He must have been successful, because we were both asleep within a few minutes.

A few hours later they brought Oliver back to us, he was ready for a meal. Go figure, he was entirely fine.

—Stacy (Mom of 1)

Place Your Baby to Sleep on Her Back

You will hear this a thousand times in every book and from every nurse, but it's worth repeating:

Place your baby to sleep on her back with nothing else in her sleeping area, because that's the best way to prevent SIDS.

SIDS, or Sudden Infant Death Syndrome, is by definition a problem whose root cause is not understood. But while scientists have yet to find exactly what causes SIDS, they have found empirically that certain behaviors dramatically reduce SIDS: most importantly, placing your baby on her back, not her stomach, and not having anything else in her sleeping area. So, no blankets, bumpers, rolled up swaddle blankets, stuffed animals, or burp cloths.

At some point, months later, your baby will start turning herself over to sleep on her stomach, and that's fine. You don't have to go in and put her back onto her back. She will have crossed into a lower risk for SIDS period anyways. By the way, you'll hear some people recommend that co-sleeping/room-sharing is or is not better for SIDS prevention. Blogs that have strong opinions one way or the other tend to interpret the data in their own biased ways. We'll give you our own brief overview.

For a long time, the American Academy of Pediatrics recommended that babies sleep in their own room in their own crib because it was viewed as safer than sharing a bed. And that has been proven empirically in observational studies. However, when co-sleeping parents who were also actively drinking or smoking while co-sleeping were subtracted from the study, the numbers were no longer comparably different. In other words, if you're drinking or smoking, definitely don't co-sleep. And if you aren't, then the safety records are comparably similar.

But then the American Academy of Pediatrics came back and said that they had found a problem with babies sleeping independently in a crib in their own room. It wasn't that babies were dying from SIDS at a higher rate in their own crib, it was that parents were choosing to soothe their babies from a couch in the living room and falling asleep there. Their babies were then suffocating underneath them. The American Academy of Pediatrics, therefore, determined that directing parents to put their babies in the parents' bedroom would decrease the number of times that parents accidentally suffocate their own babies on the couch in the living room.

Like most things in parenthood, the information is often conflicting. One thing, however, has been consistently proven over this entire time. When babies actually sleep on their backs, on their own, with no additional loose items inside their sleeping area, the SIDS rate is incredibly low. Finland has one of the lowest SIDS rates in the world, and it's because they send every new parent a cardboard box full of baby supplies and instruct the parents that babies should sleep on their backs in this bassinet-shaped cardboard box for the first several months.

A Researcher's Perspective: Back-To-Sleep Empirically Works

Studies have shown that the risk for crib death is up to ten times higher among babies who sleep on their stomachs than for those who sleep on their backs or on their sides. In many countries, the finding has led to the publication of an official recommendation by leading health agencies to put babies to sleep on their backs or on their sides and not on their stomachs.

A striking decline in the cases of inexplicable death was found in countries in which this recommendation was implemented. A recent review by a task force of the American Academy of Pediatrics indicated that since 1992, when the "back to sleep" campaign started, the number of infants sleeping on their tummy has decreased from more than 70 percent to about 20 percent, and the rate of sudden infant death syndrome has decreased by more than 40 percent. Soft sleep surfaces, soft objects, and loose bedding are additional risks factors that should be avoided.

—Dr. Avi Sadeh, *Sleeping like a Baby: A Sensitive and Sensible Approach to Solving Your Child's Sleep Problems*

Getting Back to Birth Weight

Even if your baby is born within the normal range of weight, she'll lose anywhere from five to ten percent of her weight in the first few days, as her constant supply of the nutrients from the umbilical cord are replaced with nutrients from breastfeeding. It takes several days of consistent breastfeeding before the low-volume, high-fat-content colostrum is replaced with the higher-volume breast milk.

During this time, everyone will be focused on the baby's weight. Accordingly, do whatever your pediatrician recommends you do to help your baby gain weight during these first few days—at least until she is restored to her birth weight. If your baby was born below a normal range, you'll go longer on a case-by-case basis.

In general, getting back to birth weight within the first ten days is a great milestone. There will be some pediatricians who recommend that you wake your baby up every 2-3 hours to increase the amount she is eating, and some that will say get some rest and let your baby sleep. Just default to whatever your pediatrician recommends.

An Author's Perspective: Just Take It Easy

Take it easy, but do not create bad habits. For the first 4 to 6 weeks, you are off the hook as far as serious sleep training goes. I really do not start sleep training and coaching until the babies are about 4 to 6 weeks old, depending on weight, prematurity, and other factors. Take this time to let your body recover, let your babies get used to life outside the womb, and let everyone get used to all the changes that come with birthing babies.

—Suzy Giordano, "The Baby Coach," *Twelve Hours' Sleep by Twelve Weeks Old*

A Dad's Perspective: We Started Much Later Than Most

This took us longer than it does for other babies. Our baby was in the bottom two percentile for weight, and we were doing everything possible to help him grow. It felt frantic for the first six to seven weeks, and sleep training was the farthest thing from our minds. But finally our pediatrician gave us the go ahead to focus on sleeping longer periods.

We jumped right into The Dream Feed Method around the end of month 2 and were able to finish perfectly on time by week 16!

—Gavin (Dad of three)

Establish Good Breastfeeding

Step one is establishing breastfeeding. For some moms, breastfeeding will come easily—babies will latch, milk will flow. But there are a number of complications that can arise. It's incredibly important, for a whole host of reasons, to stay focused on getting a good breastfeeding relationship established. Don't even think about anything in this book until you do.

We would offer some guidance here, however, the best solution if you're struggling is to work with experts in your area, either pediatricians or lactation consultants. With regard to the Dream Feed Method, don't worry about scheduled feedings or on-demand during these early days. Give yourself the freedom to focus on breastfeeding with no other distractions. We know of one mom who spent whole days curled up on the couch dedicated to semi-constant feeding as she worked to establish good breastfeeding habits with her son. They found their rhythm and soon progressed to more scheduled feedings, which paved the way for the Dream Feed Method. Ten weeks later they achieved their first 12-hour night!

After you reach a state of consistency with breastfeeding, you'll find it will remain very stable, and you'll then move onto sleep-training basics, including pumping and top-up bottles. Until then, give yourself the mental freedom to only focus on this one thing—helping your baby feed in the most natural, healthy way possible.

> **Jana's Perspective: There is No Schedule During the First Week. None.**
>
> Week one, the baby is strictly on the breast. They get it as much as they want, as frequently as they want. There is no schedule during the first week. None. Day or night they can have whatever they want.
>
> If mom's milk supply has not come in, then you can give the bottle. Pick a formula that you're comfortable with from the

beginning, whether it's organic or it's something your doctor might suggest or the samples from the hospital. It's okay.

—Jana Hartzell, Sleep Trainer

Start Pumping

Once you're ready, start pumping.

Don't stress about starting before you're ready. If it takes you three weeks to get there, that's fine. If you're ready to go after being home just a couple of days, that's great too. Our only guidance is that sometime in the first month you start pumping.

Only pump after feeding. You don't want to pump in between feeds because you want your milk supply to be at its fullest when your baby is ready to feed. At first, pumping right after you have fed your baby is going to produce almost no milk. But after two or three days, you may find you produce as much milk as your baby takes during a full feeding. One of the benefits of early pumping is it does stimulate additional breast milk supply, and the sooner you start producing more milk, the sooner you can use expressed milk at night.

Don't burn yourself out with pumping after every single feeding. You don't have to keep yourself up late at night by adding the process of pumping to your midnight feeding. Out of seven feedings a day, try to pump after any three or four of them. That should, after a few days, give you enough breast milk for top-up bottles and replacement bottles. In the event that this isn't the case, you may want to talk to your doctor about introducing formula. Even just an ounce here or there can bridge the gap, and adding the mixed formula directly to a bottle of breast milk will mean your baby likely won't know the difference.

American Academy of Pediatrics Guidelines: How to Pump and Store Expressed Breast Milk

Milk that is pumped should be stored in clean containers, preferably glass or rigid plastic containers or special plastic bags. Baby bottle insert bags are not strong or thick enough to protect the milk from contamination. If the milk is to be fed to the baby within 72 hours, it should be sealed and cooled immediately. If this refrigerated milk goes unused for more than 72 hours, it should be discarded. It may be frozen after up to 24 hours of refrigeration.

If you know in advance that the milk won't be used within four days, freeze it immediately. Breast milk will safely keep in your freezer for at least one month. Store it in the back of the freezer. If you have a separate deep freeze, it can be kept for about three to six months. Because the fats in human milk begin to break down over time, use the frozen milk as soon as possible.

Do not heat breast milk, formula, or bottles in a microwave oven. Microwaving overheats the milk in the center of the container. Bear in mind that heat also can destroy some of the anti-infectious, nutritious, and protective properties of breast milk.

Incidentally, when milk is thawed, its fat may separate, but that does not affect its quality. You may swirl the container gently until the milk returns to a uniform consistency.

Do not save unfinished milk from a partially consumed bottle to use at another feeding.

—American Academy of Pediatrics, *Caring for Your Baby and Young Child*

Empower Your Partner to Do a Feeding

There's no other way to say it—at some point, you have to give permission to your partner to take over a feeding. Empowerment starts with that permission. It's yours to give.

We've all been there. We know all the reasons not to. You're concerned about milk supply. You're concerned about the bottle. You love your baby and don't want to not feed him yourself.

As the non-childbearing, non-breastfeeding member of the parenting team, your partner won't be able to demand it. In fact, they won't even be able to push for it. You have to offer it. It is absolutely one of the best things you can do for your marriage, for yourself, and yes, for your baby.

You'll sleep the longest you have since before you went into labor. Your breast milk won't dry up. Your baby will still feed at the next opportunity, right from the breast, and your partner will have gained a new kind of confidence.

We're not going to push you too fast, but we have found that the earlier you take this step, the better.

It is 100 percent fine to do it the first night you're back at home.

It's 100 percent fine to do it after one week.

It's 100 percent fine to do it after one month.

Enjoy this milestone. For some of you, it will come quite easily, and you'll find we're perhaps being melodramatic. But for many more of you, giving up just one feeding will be a huge step. We promise you, your partner and your baby will both be better for it.

A Mom's Perspective: This Time Is Just Hard

I think I had this vision of what it was going to be like to be a parent. But in the first several weeks, as you well know, it's not like that at all. It's really just survival mode: you're at the beck and call of this little being who has no appreciation for you whatsoever. No recognition of you. It's just hard and thankless.

And I think I have been really mourning the life we had. What comes to mind when we think about our previous life is dinnertime: we would sit and talk in our dining room over a glass of wine and a home-cooked meal that I had been able to spend an hour making that night. Or being able to lay on the couch and watch a movie, uninterrupted, and then go to bed casually with no fear of needing to wake up at any point that night. Waking up the next morning and having all the time in the world to take showers as we please and get ready to go and do what we wanted to do.

We love our little guy. We wouldn't trade him for anything. But these first few weeks, I have been crying every single day, multiple times, about the most obscene things. I think that all of this has just been more than we anticipated, and I think that we have not quite gotten to the point where we feel this overwhelming feeling of "Oh my God, this kid is amazing. Look at him smiling at us."

We're trying, really trying, to just appreciate these early weeks of him and recognizing that he'll never be this small and vulnerable again. And trying to also just enjoy this time. But it's hard.

Especially the breastfeeding.

You know that everyone says it's so challenging and you can't quite understand why it would be so hard until you start to do it yourself. It definitely is a challenge for me. In the beginning, our son was jaundiced, and he had a tongue tie, too. I thought he was feeding just fine, but he wasn't actually eating anything.

So, he wasn't gaining weight. He dropped a bunch of weight. They were really worried. We had to supplement in the beginning a little bit with formula, which broke my heart. Yeah, it was a real challenge, and it still is a bit of a challenge in that I constantly fear that my milk supply is not quite enough for him. I have a lot of anxiety about that.

It's been two weeks and he's finally chunking up, looking healthy and happy, and I think everything is fine. I have to say it's not as magical as I expected. I had this vision of breastfeeding at one in the morning, and we were going to be bonding, and he was going to look me in the eye, and it was going to be so magical. Instead all I'm thinking is, *"Why can't you just keep your mouth on the nipple and keep sucking so we can get this over with and I can put you back in your bed?"*

But there are some magical moments, too. I'm trying to keep my eye out for them.

—Monica (New mom of one)

A Dad's Perspective: Breastfeeding Is Hard and There's Very Little I Can Do to Help

As the dad/husband, I was split between the well-being of my baby and the well-being of my wife. And I felt helpless to be there for either of them.

I wanted my Jack to eat enough and be happy and get healthy. And at the same time, I was concerned about Monica, who's being challenged with all of these difficulties of breastfeeding.

Maybe there was not enough milk production, or maybe the baby was not latching well. So, I was trying to help lift her up and keep her happy and motivated and in a good state, and at the same time deal with Jack, who I feared might not be getting enough to eat.

And we live in San Francisco, California, which is a very progressive, liberal population. So, there's a lot of breastfeed-shaming culture here. If you formula-feed your baby, or supplement with formula, you can be judged.

I think most of the women here feel a lot of pressure to meet an unrealistic expectation that your kid is somehow going to be able to easily breastfeed and only breastfeed forever and be super happy.

Although that was probably the one challenge that we expected, it was even harder than we thought.

—Lucca (Dad of 3)

A Mom's Perspective: Try Not to Stress

I put a lot of stress and pressure on myself. I was pumping all the time; I was like, "I'm going to make it to six months. Only breast milk." And I think in this process I made myself a little bit crazy. And made my husband crazy, too.

Yes, breastfeeding is generally preferable to formula feeding, if it works for you. But being a happy, rested mom is also important. I wish I hadn't put so much pressure on myself. I was crazy about it, and it was totally unnecessary.

Now, in retrospect, when I see my three-year-old eating ice cream for dinner, I realize that extra ounce of breast milk versus formula probably didn't make a bit of difference in her overall health or wellness. But nothing could have convinced me of that then.

It's senseless for me to recommend that you not drive yourself crazy. You will. All moms do. Maybe, just maybe, also try to remember when you're in the depths of it that every mom has also been there. And we made it out. And so will you.

—Kate (Mom of two)

A Dad's Perspective: Helping My Wife Sleep Six Hours

The first night home from the hospital I asked my wife, Jen, if she wanted to take one of the feedings off. I pointed out that since we didn't yet have any pumped breast milk, the baby would get a bottle of formula. She agreed, with the assumption that this would not become a regular occurrence. So, on her first night home from the hospital, Jen slept 6 hours that night, and I gave Callie a couple ounces of formula.

Jen woke up that next morning in the greatest mood, having just had 6 hours of sleep after being up the vast majority of the previous 72 hours. And so on the second night, we agreed we'd do it again. Of course, we had the same outcome: Jen felt amazing (and Callie returned to nursing without issue first thing that morning).

So, we kept it going, and within a couple of days, Jen had a little bit of extra breast milk pumped, so I used that in the bottle that I gave.

Jen's milk still came in. Breastfeeding still went well. All that happened is that Callie got a few ounces of formula at night. And Jen got some much-needed sleep.

—Jason (Dad of 3)

2. Weeks Two Through Six: Use Top-Up Bottles

Goals:

✓ **Establish top-up bottles**

✓ **Establish 3-hour scheduled feedings**

✓ **Lock in the 7:00 a.m. feeding**

✓ **Lock in the 7:00 p.m. bedtime feeding**

Establish Top-Up Bottles

As we've already discussed, many parents, warned about nipple confusion, never introduce a bottle until they're ready to return to work or otherwise need to start offering bottles during the day. And then they're surprised to learn that their baby isn't "taking to the bottle."

This is entirely preventable. Just start with top-up bottles early on, as soon as successful breastfeeding has been established, and you can be assured that your baby will learn to feed both from the breast and from the bottle.

The Dream Feed Method will ensure you do exactly this, as it is core to our approach. You should aim to begin introducing these bottles somewhere between two and six weeks (and as you've heard us say before, earlier is better).

A Researcher's Perspective: There Is No Need to Fear That Using a Bottle Will Cause the Milk Supply to Dry Up

I have never understood why feeding should be seen as only fully breast or only fully bottle. If a woman is producing good quality breast milk but in slightly inadequate volumes, why not complement it with an alternative feed? Some mothers will find that if they supplement from the bottle immediately following the breastfeed then the baby settles well, sleeps deeply, and awakens to feed efficiently at the next mealtime.

This pattern can be made a little more specific. The supply of breast milk tends to decrease in the late afternoon. While the morning feeds may be adequate for the baby's needs, by late afternoon the milk supply may be insufficient to supply the baby's whole requirement. Because the top-up bottle is given after breastfeeding, the baby's demand for breast milk is not reduced. There is no need to fear that using a bottle will cause the milk supply to dry up.

—Brian Symon, M.D.

The 7:00 p.m. Top-Up Bottle

At that 7:00 p.m. feeding, you'll want to give your baby a full feeding from the breast, followed by as much expressed breast milk (or formula) from a bottle as he wants. He'll let you know when he's had enough by refusing the nipple. Many babies will be sleepy for this feeding and may fall asleep on the bottle. As you get to know your baby's capacity for this feed, you'll start to play around with waking him just enough to get that last little bit of milk in. This is just as much art as science.

In the first few weeks, this top-up bottle may be as little as an ounce or two, but that will progress to four or five ounces or more as your baby grows. The top-up bottle may also help if you're struggling to lock in the 7:00 p.m. bedtime because your baby will be more full. And when your baby is full, you'll find he'll fall asleep and more easily stay asleep.

Three-Hour Scheduled Feedings

The first milestone for this stage is to create some regularity with feedings, ultimately aiming for a feed every 3 hours.

7:00 a.m.–>10:00 a.m.–>1:00 p.m.–>4:00 p.m.–>
7:00 p.m.–>10:00 p.m.–>1:00 a.m.–>4:00 a.m.

Measure each scheduled feeding from the beginning of the feeding, regardless of how long it takes.

To achieve consistency with the 3-hour schedule, you will need to hold your baby off until the next feeding. As you work to stretch toward those 3-hour increments, we encourage you to use every trick in the book. This isn't the time to worry about your baby's ability (or lack thereof) to self-soothe.

It's okay to use a rocker that has a vibrator built-in. It's okay to pick up your baby and rock her. Pacifiers? Absolutely. Whatever it takes to hold off until the beginning of the new feeding cycle. Establishing the 3-hour cycle sets the foundation for being able to do everything else.

Your baby will adjust. She'll learn to take in more food in order to last 3 hours. She'll learn not to cry when her stomach is still half-full because the 3-hour schedule presents a comfortable, reliable predictability.

(As noted before: Your 3-hour schedule can start at any time. There's nothing magical about this timing we use, but for the sake of simplicity, we'll use the schedule that starts at 7:00 a.m. throughout the book. If you choose to start at a different time, just adjust everything accordingly.)

A Pediatrician's Perspective: You Make the Baby Wait Three Hours Between Feedings

When the baby has slept 3 hours, two nights in a row, then you need to define that as the normal, expected nighttime sleep interval. That means that if the baby wakes up at 2 hours and 45 minutes, you don't feed the baby, you don't touch the baby, you don't talk to the baby, you don't plug the baby with a pacifier. You make the baby wait 3 hours between feedings.

—Eileen Aicardi, M.D.

A Mom's Perspective: Three-Hour Feedings

One of the things that I learned very quickly was the difference between a full meal and snacking. And so I really did work hard to get my son on at least a 2- to 3-hour schedule as opposed to letting him feed every hour. Once he regained his birth weight, he became an even more efficient feeder. I had more milk, he was happier, and he slept longer. Everything just fell into a groove. Our main focus in those first four weeks was getting him to a 3-hour schedule as much as possible.

—Divya (Mom of one)

A Half-Full Stomach

The big early difference between a baby who makes it to a 3-hour scheduled feeding and one that doesn't is whether she is capable of remaining content even when her stomach is only half-full. The baby that makes it to 3-hour scheduled feedings with regularity has learned that when her stomach is half-full, there is nothing to worry about. There's no discomfort. And it's only when her stomach is nearly empty that she cries out for food.

The baby that struggles to get to 3-hour scheduled feedings cries out when she is anything other than full. This is the baby that snacks instead of eating full meals, using feeding for comfort instead of sustenance.

Getting to the 3-hour scheduled feeding milestone is so important because this is the step that helps babies learn the difference between a half-filled stomach and an empty stomach. When they move toward longer and longer sleep periods at night, you want your baby to feel comfortable sleeping another couple of hours when her stomach is only half-empty.

That's why the key to getting to the 3-hour schedule is not crossing your fingers and hoping your baby magically gets there on her own. Nor is it using some harsh self-discipline where you must watch her cry. In fact, it's quite the opposite.

Go ahead and provide the comfort that your baby is seeking at the 90-minute or 2-hour mark. Hold her, rock her, cuddle her, sing her songs, or use your vibrating chair. Help her learn that there are ways to feel soothed beyond constant feeding. She'll quickly adjust as her body adapts to the rhythm of constantly receiving this feeding at the 3-hour mark.

As the regularity sets in, you can almost set your clock to your baby's needs. She'll be so accustomed to having the feeding every 3 hours she will let you know exactly at that 3-hour mark that it's now time to feed.

People in the on-demand feeding camp argue that you shouldn't let your baby feel distress this early on. And the traditional sleep-trainer camp has provided a stark contrast advocating that you just let your baby cry. Hopefully, like many other strategies in this book, you will find this to be a nice middle ground that helps you achieve progress in preparing your baby to sleep well while not forcing either of you to endure long bouts of crying.

Daytime Top-Up Bottles Can Help

If you're still struggling to get your baby to 3-hour scheduled feedings, it's worth checking to see that she's eating enough.

As a rule of thumb, your baby should easily be able to last an hour or more for every ounce that she takes in. If she takes three ounces of milk, you can feel very confident she can last 3 hours or more. If she is taking only an ounce-and-a-half, she is going to struggle to get to 3 hours.

To find out how much milk your baby is getting at any given feeding, switch from breastfeeding to bottle-feeding with either formula or expressed breast milk just once. While we're huge advocates of breastfeeding, it's very difficult to know how much milk your baby is taking from the breast whereas the bottle tells you exactly. And one bottle won't do anything at all to stop your breastfeeding progress.

There might be two reasons your baby will only be taking an ounce-and-a-half of milk at this point.

First, check to see if you're producing enough milk to keep your baby satisfied. If you're not, use the top-up bottle method to give her a little bit of extra milk at each feeding. Top-up bottles are wonderful for supporting breastfeeding while still making sure that your baby has enough nutrients in her to power her through the day.

If you're pumping after each feeding to store up enough expressed breast milk for use in the top-up bottles, then that extra pumping will also help stimulate additional milk production. If you don't yet have any expressed breast milk stored up, a little bit of formula in the top-up bottle will help fill your baby's stomach so she can make it 3 hours. And a little bit of formula mixed in with a focus on breastfeeding won't do anything to dilute all the value that breastfeeding is providing to your baby.

If you find you are producing plenty of milk but your baby is still not making it 3 hours, it could be that she's simply not accustomed to taking in a large enough quantity at any given feeding. This is the snacking pattern.

Your baby is used to eating small amounts and requesting more food soon thereafter. You can change this pattern by stretching out the amount of time between feedings. If your baby is used to taking about an ounce-and-a-half every 90 minutes, just hold her off for an extra 15 minutes each day. You will likely have to actively soothe her for those 15 minutes, but it's a small adjustment. Your baby can get there (and so can you). To go from a 90-minute scheduled feeding to a 3-hour scheduled feeding can take you a full week of adding 15 minutes each day. And each day that you add 15 minutes, she'll adjust by taking slightly larger feedings.

Lock In the 7:00 a.m. Feeding

No matter what happens in the middle of the night, you should always start the day at the same exact time. Again, we say 7:00 a.m., but really it can be any time that works for you and for your family. The important thing is to lock in the same time to start the day consistently.

You want your baby to always be accustomed to getting up at the same time for a full feeding from the breast only. By enforcing a consistent 7:00 a.m. start as the first feeding of the day, it also allows the rest of your day to have a measure of consistency, so you can more easily stick to a 3-hour schedule.

Cluster Feed in the Late Afternoon

You want your baby to learn to take in twice the amount of milk before going to sleep as he does during a normal feeding. And then again twice as much when he wakes up. This is a learned behavior that your baby can pick up as early as the first few weeks.

After establishing a regular, 3-hour schedule, your baby is accustomed to waiting until her stomach is fairly empty before filling it up completely at the breast.

Right from the start, you can make an exception to this with the 4:00 p.m. to 7:00 p.m. period. During this time, it is totally fine to cluster feed, which means you can feed him once or twice in the middle of the 3-hour period. By doing a cluster feed at, say, 5:30 p.m., your breast milk supply will still be depleted when you go to feed at 7:00 p.m. You'll still feed by breast at the 7:00 p.m. feeding, but you'll know that your baby could probably take more and you'll offer a top-up bottle.

The goal is that at the completion of the 7:00 p.m. feeding, plus the supplementary top-up, your baby has more milk in her than usual, giving her just a little bit more fuel to last longer into the night.

As an additional benefit, many babies, especially in the first eight weeks, have a "witching hour" sometime between 4:00 p.m. and 7:00 p.m. Knowing you can simply feed your baby whenever he gets fussy during this time will remove a lot of stress from both of you.

Jana's Perspective: Cluster Feeding Settles Them Down

Cluster feeding is giving the baby as much milk, from the breast, as possible between 4:00 p.m. and 7:00 p.m. to prepare them for the night. That's also the witching hour when babies tend to be fussier; they want to be on the breast, but sometimes the milk is just not there. When it's time to get the baby ready for bed and you've done the last breastfeeding for the evening, you give them a bottle to top them off. It's just that last little bit that settles them. Sometimes, in the beginning, it's just an ounce—not even an ounce. It can be two ounces, whatever they need to get comfortable and go to sleep.

—Jana Hartzell, Sleep Trainer

Lock In the 7:00 p.m. Bedtime

It is very important to get this 7:00 p.m. bedtime feed locked in correctly right from the beginning. Getting your baby to sleep from 7:00 p.m. to 10:00 p.m. is one of the most important milestones in early sleep training.

The key to putting your baby down smoothly is reducing all stimulation and creating a very consistent pattern. No matter where you do the bedtime routine, whether it's in the nursery, your own bedroom, or the living room, make sure it's a quiet environment with no interruptions. This means keeping the television off, dimming the lights, and asking your partner to speak quietly if he needs to come talk to you. It's easy to judge the environment from our adult perspective and assume it's "quiet enough" or "dark enough." But remember that for a young infant who has just only recently emerged from the 24-7 consistency of the womb, the real world is still taking some getting used to. You'll find that by designing a more ideal bedtime environment, your baby will transition to sleep more easily.

To help achieve this, plan ahead. The parent who is doing bedtime should have everything at the ready—the baby is changed, the swaddle is snug, the bed is arranged, the white noise machine is switched on, and the lights are already low. No one else is in the room, and the top-off bottle is already warm and within arm's reach. If this entire preamble process takes twenty minutes, which is not uncommon, that's fine too, as long as it's happening in a sleep-like environment with no one else coming in and out of the room.

As you sit down to provide your 7:00 p.m. feeding from the breast, reduce the dimmer switch on your lamp to almost nothing. As much as possible, you should be breastfeeding in the dark, burping in the dark, and then offering the top-off bottle in the dark. It's tempting to do the feeding yourself and then ask your partner to do the top-off bottle and putting down process, but even that little transition is enough to stimulate your baby and prolong this process significantly.

If you can get everything done in a quiet room with no other distractions other than the white noise machine in the dimmest of light, then the bedtime pattern will be established and soon enough it will turn into a very predictable process. In fact, doing it this way is what allows you to achieve one of the all-time most wonderful feats of early sleep training: the ability to put your baby down in her crib drowsy but still awake and walk away knowing she'll fall asleep on her own. Many, many parents never get there, nor even think it's possible. But if you're really consistent at creating this low stimulation environment and following a set pattern night after night, you can get there.

If you're struggling at all, one final little trick is try moving the bedtime earlier—not later—which may feel counterintuitive. Your baby may be struggling to fall asleep because she's overtired. Some babies can fall asleep quite easily at 6:30 p.m. but will put up a fight after 7:00 p.m.

Don't Lose Hope in the Sixth Week

For some of you, the sixth week (give or take a couple of weeks) may feel like an extreme low point. Don't lose hope. This can be a particularly tough time for a few different reasons, and the good news is it's also about to get much better.

First, let's address why so many parents struggle around this time, and then we'll talk about what to do. There are two big reasons: one affecting your baby and one affecting you.

Around the sixth week is when gas is at its most painful for some babies. It's very difficult for your baby to link together sleep cycles or to self-soothe back to sleep when he's in pain from gas. While there are lots of suggestions, and we offer a bunch of them below, the reality is your baby's body is building itself quite quickly, and this results in the production of a great deal of gas that his body doesn't yet know how to deal with. There is only so much you can do.

For babies that are colicky—ever so helpfully defined as "unexplained crying for more than 3 hours a day and more than 3 weeks in a row"—often gas is the root cause. Before we give you a bunch of suggestions on dealing with this, here is the fantastic news. The whole issue is about to solve itself.

Gas, for most babies, goes away sometime in the second month pretty much no matter what you do. By all means, try the suggestions below, but if we or anyone else had a more conclusive, specific recommendation to make, we would. The reality is most parents try some combination of these approaches, the gas goes away on its own, and yet they attribute the success to whatever method they last tried.

All of the suggestions below don't really hurt, so you might as well see what works for your baby. But remember, you just need to hang in there a little bit longer; your baby will work this out for himself quite soon.

Suggestions for Dealing with Gas

- Make sure you burp him often. Your baby can't burp himself yet. All the various methods (lightly twirling your baby, firmly patting him on the back, resting him over your knee, sitting him up on the changing table, resting him over your shoulder, etc.) can work. Just make sure you're getting at least one burp for every feeding and preferably a couple if they're small.

- Do the bicycle (for your baby). A lot of baby whisperers spend some time rotating the baby's legs clockwise, counter-clock-wise, and in a bicycle motion, all in an attempt to move those gas bubbles. In fact, the gas bubbles are tiny micro bubbles, and what you're actually doing is helping them combine into a single larger bubble that can then be burped out. Like all the other suggestions, a little extra movement on the changing table is definitely not going to hurt. And if you find it's giving your baby better or bigger burps, by all means continue.

- Gas drops. Many mothers swear by them. And a lactation consultant we've worked with points out that a benefit of the gas drops is their sweetness, which will cause a writhing, crying, baby to pause and relax for a few moments. Gas needs relaxed muscles to pass itself through the body, so often the momentary pause in crying will move things along.

- Gripe water. This can work similarly to gas drops.

The second big reason this period of time may be a low point for you is that the rush of energy that has helped power you through since giving birth is now beginning to wear off. Your body (and even your partner's body) has been pumped with hormones to help you survive this early period of being parents. It is nature's way of saying, "This is hard, we're going to put a little more gas in your tank." These hormones tend to recede around the sixth week and with them, your superpowers.

So, with all the empathy in the world (because we've all been there), we wanted to just make sure you know at this crucial moment that all of us who got our babies sleeping from dusk till dawn before the fourth month had low points around this time.

Our babies were colicky. Our babies were "hard" babies. Our babies were gassy. And we ran out of both hope and energy all around the sixth week. But we got through it, and so will you.

If you enter this period of time feeling like nothing has worked so far and then harboring secret animosity toward your new mommy friends who don't seem to be struggling, take a big deep breath. Get ready to dig in. Over the next few weeks, no matter what point you're at now, you're going to be able to make a lot of progress. And because your baby is actively developing in new and exciting ways, what previously wasn't working is now going to start to work.

You can do this.

A Mom's Perspective: Getting Him to Fall Asleep on His Own Was, Shall We Say, Challenging

It's quickly become Dave's responsibility to feed Oliver at 7:00 p.m. with a bottle and to put him to bed. And David was also mostly in charge from 7:00 p.m. until 10:00 p.m., when I would breastfeed him. If Oliver wasn't going down easily, then he held him, rocked him, shushed him, whatever needed to happen. I actually went to bed shortly after pumping at about 7:30 p.m.

There were many nights where Dave did all of the right things to settle Oliver for bed. He'd put him in the bassinet and tiptoe out of the nursery. Then we'd check the baby monitor only to find our most feared sight: Oliver with his eyes wide open. It would only be a matter of minutes before we'd need to go in and soothe him.

I'd read those books that talk about teaching your infant to self-soothe and fall asleep by themselves in the bassinet in the first six weeks. And I had to ask: what infant does that? Mine did not. If he was not asleep when we laid him down in his bassinet, chances were he would definitely not put himself to sleep. He'd humor us for about four minutes before the screaming began.

It's only in retrospect that I see that this was just a tough period. Oliver was a different baby three weeks later, and what had once been so incredibly hard and stressful—verging on hopeless—finally started working.

—Stacy (Mom of 1)

A Mom's Perspective: Month One, Don't Worry About Bad Habits

Looking back, I was way too concerned early on with "bad habits." I spent a week being very unhappy and stressed out, because I thought I was teaching him bad sleep habits. Like letting him sleep on me during the day was maybe going to teach him that that's how we sleep—we sleep on mom. And that's so unsustainable; I can't have him sleeping on me all the time.

I think that my fear of instilling bad habits took some of the enjoyment out of those early weeks, because I couldn't let go of all this information in my head. Everything seemed like a monumental choice. I felt on edge about letting him be a newborn baby and having those moments with me. It feels sad, even now, to say this.

Once I finally got over the fear of instilling bad self-soothing habits, I enjoyed things a lot more. Recently, we've had a couple of days where I've binge-watched Downton Abbey while he sleeps on me, and it's been pretty great. Truly great, actually.

That's the stuff that I'm going to look back on some day and really cherish, you know? Just these quiet moments together.

—Megan (Mom of one)

A Mom's Perspective: He Can Take a Lot More Milk That I Thought He Could

When you actually go to the point of giving your baby as much milk as she'll take, you might be a little surprised by how much that ends up being. For our daughter, it was far more than I ever thought. It was crazy to see Emma take down an eight-ounce bottle of milk before going to sleep. I was only pumping about four ounces at a time, and yet she could drink eight. It was really intimidating.

It caused me to ask all of these questions: "If I am not producing that much, then am I not able to get her what she needs? What does that mean for the rest of the day?" It spirals into all of these fears and concerns.

That was a moment for me to take a step back, and realize that this wasn't that big of a deal. This wasn't about me and my breast milk. It was about Emma and her having enough food in her belly to sleep through the night. We found that the right amount of milk for her at nighttime was twice the amount that I would have been able to feed her from my breasts in a single feeding. And that was okay.

—Jeanne (Mom of 2)

3. Preempt Crying with Dream Feeds: Weeks Four Through Eight

Goals:

✓ **Establish dream feeds**

✓ **Give up one feeding to your partner**

✓ **Hold off until the 7:00 a.m. feeding**

✓ **Skip a night changing**

Establish Dream Feeds

Now it's time for the real fun to begin. Introducing dream feeds is what's going to take your baby from waking every few hours to going longer and longer stretches of sleep.

Up until this point, you've been in reaction mode, trying to help your baby stretch to 3 hours between feedings. Now you're going to preempt those awakenings with a dream feed. There's nothing special about waiting until exactly five weeks to get started with dream feeds. In general, we recommend that mom and baby first successfully recover from the birth and any complications that arose. We also want to make sure that you have successfully established breastfeeding. For some, that will be a quick process, and for others it may involve quite a bit of work and perseverance. Either way, take the time to establish your breastfeeding before jumping into dream feeds.

Some parents, especially experienced parents, can be ready for dream feeds as early as a week after birth if there were zero complications, breast milk came in quickly, a good latch was formed, and the baby regained her birth weight. For others, it may take three or four weeks before all that comes together.

There is nothing about dream feeds that will in any way inhibit any of those early goals. However, we are cognizant that a sleep-training book and active pediatrician advice are too many cooks in the kitchen. We generally prefer that the guidance in this book stay on the sidelines until you have a thumbs-up from your pediatrician and are personally feeling comfortable.

Now on to the specifics of how to do a dream feed.

We lightly recommend you start dream feeds from the bottle rather than the breast. While we are all big proponents of breastfeeding, the dream feed takes a little practice to get right, and it just seems to work more smoothly with a bottle. Of course, it's just a recommendation. Feel free to start with breastfeeding for your dream feeds, and if it's working, there is no need to change!

Assuming you've already started top-up bottles at the 7:00 p.m. feeding, you should be adept at feeding both from the breast and from the bottle.

Go to your baby before he is likely to wake up.

Keep the room as dim as possible.

Gently lift him from the bassinet and cradle him so that he remains horizontal. You'll leave him fully swaddled.

Take the nipple of the bottle or your breast and gently tickle his upper lip.

Once your baby opens his mouth, gently insert the nipple and watch with amazement as he establishes a latch and starts sucking.

If you struggle the first few times to get him to latch, try allowing a few drops of milk to wet his lips while continuing to tickle his upper lip. Almost all parents can get there with a little bit of persistence.

At about 70 percent though the feeding, you'll want to pause for a burp. If you're going to do a diaper change, this is also when you'll want to do that. As we mentioned earlier, you'll want to avoid changing wet diapers, as this is sure to wake your baby fully. Typically the absorbency of modern diapers and the protection of ointment are enough to prevent any rashes. Also, resist un-swaddling your baby just to check. If your baby is not showing any agitation from a slightly wet or soiled diaper, there's no need to inspect it.

If you do need to change the diaper, make sure you are using a type of swaddle that allows for opening the leg area without completely removing the swaddle. It's also helpful to keep the light as dim as possible and directed away from the face. Move quickly and try to get your baby re-swaddled and off the changing table before he wakes too much.

Then go back to feeding the remaining 30 percent of the bottle (or however much he is interested in taking).

In the best of scenarios, your baby didn't actually wake up fully. He finished his last little bit of milk, and you were able to return him to his bassinet without a peep. But even if your baby woke at times, he'll likely remain drowsy and will easily be soothed back to sleep.

Of course, there will be times when your baby will wake completely, and the dream feed will be a dream no longer. That may happen relatively often in the beginning. In this case, nothing has been lost by attempting the dream feed. You still needed to do the feeding at approximately that time anyway. With a little practice and extra attention focused on not introducing any stimulation, you should be able to get more and more consistent with keeping your baby from waking up fully during the dream feed.

Once you get the hang of it with a bottle, try it from the breast as well if you would like. Some mothers have good luck with this and some don't. It's really a case-by-case basis. If it takes you a long time to let down or your baby doesn't suck while laying horizontally you may find that the dream feed doesn't work as well from the breast. Also, be careful of underfeeding during the dream feed. If you're feeding from the breast and he's taking less than he otherwise would have taken, then you need to make sure you supplement with a top-off bottle or stick to a purely bottle-based dream feed.

A Dad's Perspective: How I Do the Dream Feed

I don't wake him in any way—the usual temptation to speak to him or stroke his cheek is something I am careful to avoid doing. When I walk into the nursery, I'm sort of in "stealth mode"—I keep everything dark. And just ever so gently lift him out of his crib, keeping him lying horizontal across my forearm instead of lifting him up to my shoulder like I might normally do when he's awake.

I carefully settle into the rocking chair; the bottle is already within reach. In the bottle is warmed breast milk, and I usually have a second bottle with formula in case I feel he needs a top-up. When I rub the bottle nipple against his upper lip, like magic, he opens his mouth and starts reflexively sucking—but he's still not really awake. His eyes are closed shut, and he's very relaxed.

I settle in and watch him drain the bottle. When there is still an ounce or two left, I take a quick break and bring him to my shoulder so that he can burp. He can semi-wake at this point, but he remains so drowsy that he really only rubs his face into my shoulder before conking out completely again. At this time, I bring him back down into the crook of my arm and let him finish the breast milk bottle. Once he's done with that, I offer him the second, top-up bottle until he spits out the nipple and turns his face away. I don't typically burp him again at this point. He's dead asleep, so I'm not concerned about gas pains bothering him.

I always skip the diaper change for the dream-feed and have never had an issue with diaper rash or apparent discomfort on his part. This way he stays swaddled and sleeping peacefully. Returning him back to his bassinet is a piece of cake—it's like he never knew the whole feeding even happened. And the best part: what could easily have been an hour-long feed and soothe (rinse and repeat) situation turned into a consistent 15-20 minute feeding (no soothing required).

—Dave (Dad of 1)

A Mom's Perspective: The Key Is Enough Milk

When we did the dream feed, our daughter almost always woke up. But because we preempted her crying—and had the bottle already there—she woke up in a calm state, which seemed to make it easier for her to fall back to sleep. The key for us was ensuring we offered enough milk. Each time, we went into the nursery with more than we thought she would take, so we never ran out. This meant she was nice and full by the end of the feed, and easily sunk back into a deep sleep.

—Caroline (Mom of two)

Give Up One Feeding to Your Partner

If breastfeeding is going well, if pumping is going well, if top-up bottles are going well, then it is time to hand over one feeding to your spouse.

Equipped with a bottle of pumped breast milk or formula, your spouse can take over one of the middle-of-the-night dream feeds. Early on, give yourself the gift of sleep by letting your partner take over a feeding. Your baby will do just fine. Your partner will do just fine. You won't cause nipple confusion. You won't slow your own milk production. All that will happen is that one feeding out of seven will be from a bottle. And you'll be assured one long, revitalizing, stretch of sleep each night. It'll feel better than your best spa day.

It's totally normal for mothers on the Dream Feed Method in the second month to sleep 6 hours in a row consistently, not because their baby is necessarily sleeping 6 hours in a row, but because the mothers switch off feedings with their spouse.

Now, you may have to wake up to pump in the middle of the night. And certainly do so if your body is telling you it wants to. But even pumping from bed for 15 minutes and then immediately going back to sleep will be the best rest you've had in a month.

For some of you, this will be very easy, and for others, this will be a bigger decision. All too often, new mothers inadvertently push their partners away. Or less bluntly said, they don't invite them to participate more. No matter how equal the relationship is between the mother and father, it typically falls on the mom to empower her partner to take on a greater level of involvement.

A Researcher's Perspective: Let the Breastfeeding Mother Go to Bed Early

One pattern that I am particularly fond of is where the breast-feeding mother is able to go to bed early. She may be in bed by 8:00 p.m. or 9:00 p.m. Often the father will stay up, and he may be able to give a full bottle-feed at some time between 9:00 p.m. and 11:00 p.m. The mother sleeps through this feed, but then provides the next feed, as a breastfeed, after a block of sleep that may have been between 4 and 6 hours long. I find that this approach provides good support for the mother's rest, sense of well-being and, ultimately, her breastfeeding.

—Brian Symon, M.D.

A Mom's Perspective: For Us, the Bottle Worked Best

The first night we tried a dream feed was a total disaster. Oliver would not wake up enough to breastfeed. We had him completely out of his swaddle, we were tickling his feet, but he wouldn't wake. He was completely passed out.

So Dave took the bottle of breast milk from the fridge, warmed it up, and gave Oliver a dream feed with the bottle while I pumped. It was so much more efficient on all fronts.

At first, I was a little put out that Oliver took better to the bottle. But the next morning I had no issues breastfeeding. And that first night was really a turning point for Dave. Suddenly he had a role to play (beyond diaper duty). He was, of course, great at it—and I got a little extra sleep. Win-win.

—Stacy (Mom of 1)

A Mom's Perspective: My Husband Is an Equal Partner

One of our biggest learnings is the importance of equal commitment from both partners throughout this process.

When I originally read this book, I remembered how much it talked about the need for the partner to be involved—for them to feed the bottle, etc. We've realized it's not just about helping out with a bottle in the middle of the night, it's about fully sharing in this goal of helping our baby sleep through the night.

And that's how it should be, because Saura sleeping through the night benefits both of us. We're happier. Our marriage is happier. Everything clicked into place and started to work again for us.

I think, in a lot of cases, the classic sleep training usually falls to the mother. She's the one who's still getting up for every night feeding. She's the one who knows exactly when he needs to eat, and she's the one who probably ultimately makes the decision to do cry-it-out. For many of my girlfriends, that's when the husband swoops in to save the day, letting the mom check into a hotel for the night while he stays home and listens to the baby cry.

Our scenario looked very different: we had conversations every day about how Saura slept the night before. We talked about how much she ate and when. And together we'd decide on a game plan for the upcoming night. It's never been my decision or Rupesh's decision about moving back the clock. It's always a joint decision, and he is equally invested because he's the one who is physically doing it. We both have a shared understanding of how all of this works together. That's been huge for us.

I think it's also probably overflowed into the rest of our approach to parenting, because sleep is such a big, early challenge for parents. It's kind of a huge accomplishment for both of us, and it's awesome that we're able to share this experience.

—Nisha

Hold Off Until the 7:00 a.m. Feeding

7:00 a.m. is going to be the first feeding of the day. And, partners, this is likely going to be your responsibility from now through the rest of the Dream Feed Method. Your baby is not necessarily going to sleep until 7:00 a.m. Your baby might wake up at 6:00 a.m. or 6:30 a.m. or 6:45 a.m., but your job is to be the sole person responsible for soothing her until 7:00 a.m. And you need to soothe her without feeding her.

You can use any technique you want—rocking, vibrating chairs, pacifiers, and so forth—as long as you hold that baby off until 7:00 a.m. At 7:00 a.m., she will get a full feeding from mom from the breast.

Why the partner and not mom?

Holding off until the 7:00 a.m. feeding is the hardest part of the Dream Feed Method. We've moved this hard work from 4:00 a.m., where most parents get stuck, but it's still hard. You're asking your baby to wait 15 minutes, when she's used to immediate gratification. Once your baby smells mommy, with breasts full of milk, her crying is going to ratchet up three levels.

Let mom sleep until 7:00 a.m. You can do this.

A Mom's Perspective: Getting the Morning Right Took Weeks

I really didn't feel that we got our mornings back until after we finished the full Dream Feed Method. In fact, I was convinced the method wasn't working because, during the second month, he would wake at seemingly random times in the morning. What worked for us was staying consistent.

We would sit next to his bed and soothe him without picking him up (only because he assumed we were going to nurse him if we picked him up). He didn't cry, and sometimes we'd sit there for an hour and half to make it to 7:00 a.m. Other days he would sleep right to 7:00 a.m., and we'd have to wake him up. After a few weeks of doing this, he would wake up and chat happily to himself in his crib until we came to get him. My advice is to keep holding on even if it feels less scheduled than you think!

—Emily (Mom of 1)

There's No Need for Wailing

We know that it might feel difficult to apply what we're saying here to your real-world scenario. How do you know when it's time to "give in" to your baby...and when it's okay to hold off that extra five minutes to make your 7:00 a.m. goal? We fully recognize that these minutes each morning will not be your favorite. It will, at times, feel like hard work—and you'll probably wonder if you're taking the right approach to this whole "sleep thing." A lot of the parents we work with reference this experience as their first taste of the age-old adage: "This pains me more than it does you." Parenting, we all quickly learn, is about doing the right thing for your child in the long run—even if it's inconvenient or simply less pleasing in the moment.

But if you find yourself genuinely struggling with those minutes each morning, we encourage you to take a step back and consider your sleep-training alternatives. Most parents who never initiate the Dream Feed Method will ultimately find themselves facing some version of the cry-it-out method later on. As the name suggests, this will involve crying—and for a much longer period of time than we're talking about between 6:30 a.m. and 7:00 a.m.

Under the cry-it-out method, this period of crying is when your baby learns to self-soothe, breaking his associations of external soothing and nighttime feedings as a prerequisite for sleep.

The Dream Feed Method doesn't work this way. The Dream Feed Method coaxes your baby to longer sleep periods before those associations are established. There's no pattern to break. Since your baby is too young (first four months) to have established any patterns, there's no need to "learn" self-soothing by wailing.

But the coaxing is important.

With the Dream Feed Method, you're asking your baby to go a little bit longer each night, starting with slightly more milk in the belly and lasting slightly longer. We're only making small incremental extensions. At the end of that last sleep period, sometime around 6:00 a.m. to 7:00 a.m., you're only asking your baby to go an extra ten minutes or so. Hold him off by soothing him, rocking him, using a pacifier, vibrating chair, or absolutely anything you want except feeding. You're just trying to get him to go an extra ten minutes without feeding.

Ideally, this holding off period won't be tremendously painful on either of you. But nor should you expect that you'll get your baby completely calm before his feeding. Because his stomach is nearly empty, he's not just going to accept few minutes of swaying as the "end all be all" and then comfortably lie there. He's ready to eat, and you're asking him to be patient because there's still 10 percent left in his stomach. These mornings will take effort, but soon they'll be a distant memory.

Is there an exception to all of this? Is there a scenario in which you shouldn't hold your baby off those extra minutes? If his stomach is truly empty, no amount of soothing is going to help. You'll recognize the difference in his cries—they will transcend the complain cry and escalate to frantic wail. Your baby's beyond hungry and wants to eat immediately.

If you find yourself in the midst of this kind of crying, there's no need to wait one minute, five minutes, anything. Just feed him.

The Dream Feed Method requires that you consistently, night after night, diligently try and hold your baby off for an extra ten minutes. You're not going to succeed every time. You're going to let your baby guide you. If you put in those extra ten minutes of effort without causing too much pain on either of you, you've succeeded and can move forward with another ten minutes the next night. If it is causing a tremendous amount of pain either on the baby or on you, then you retreat by ten minutes. Try again the next night and pay close attention to that Dream Feed. Patiently let your baby take as much milk as he can; this will help him make those extra fifteen minutes come morning.

There will be a sweet spot for your baby where the gains seem almost effortless. This may happen after many weeks of struggling and plateauing, but all of a sudden you'll find yourselves making 10-, 20-, 30-minute gains every single night. Many babies reach this sweet spot somewhere between the 7th and 12th week, so be on the lookout for it.

If you're struggling, keep trying. Don't assume something's wrong; just be patient. The Dream Feed Method parallels parenting in general, it's more marathon than sprint. Settle in, do your best to maintain a steady pace, and you'll get there.

Night Changings

This might sound counterintuitive for most—especially brand new parents—but a pro-tip of parents who have succeeded with the Dream Feed Method is to skip a few (if not all) nighttime diaper changes.

Some may fear the dreaded onset of diaper rash but, in our experience, this just hasn't been the case. Diapers today are so advanced that their material effectively holds the moisture away from the baby's bottom. Coupled with a liberal layer of ointment, your baby's skin will be protected. Of course, every baby is different (and so is his skin), so experiment with skipping changes— see how far you can go—and if you find you must incorporate a change or two in the middle of the night, practice doing so as efficiently as possible.

> **An Author's Perspective: Don't Interrupt Sleep for a Nighttime Change**
>
> Nighttime diapers are important because you want to change the baby's diaper only if she has pooped. Changing wet diapers all night will interrupt sleep for both you and the baby.
>
> —Suzy Giordano, "The Baby Coach," *Twelve Hours' Sleep by Twelve Weeks Old*

A Pediatrician's Perspective: Just Goop Up That Little Bottom and Don't Worry About It

Toward the end of the first month, you do not need to change the diaper at every feeding. You goop the baby's little bottom up with diaper ointment. And you don't worry about it.

After the first month, most babies either slow down or completely stop the number of bowel movements they have at night. The problem with nighttime diaper changes with every feed is it wakes the baby up and then you have to feed the baby again to soothe him. Then, he'll likely have another bowel movement, and you'll be back where you started.

When you think you hear the baby poop, the problem with what you hear is that it doesn't necessarily tell you how much poop there is. Sometimes it is just gas, and others maybe there's just a little dime-sized worth of poop. That's not going to bother your baby. If your baby's not wailing about a full diaper, you don't need to worry about it.

—Eileen Aicardi, M.D.

A Mom's Perspective: Skipping Changing at the 3:30 Feeding

At first we did change Oliver with every feeding—it just seemed like what we were supposed to do. But before long, we simply stopped changing Oliver for his dream feed (it was so much easier—he was sound asleep).

Instead, I'd change him during the feed preceding the dream feed (since he would usually already be awake), and we'd leave him in his diaper until morning.

> Now, looking back, I realize how silly I was to have ever worried about the number of hours he spent between changings. Because, of course, the point of the Dream Feed Method was to help Oliver sleep 12 straight hours a night... and we don't want to wake him midway through that night for a diaper change he hasn't asked for!
>
> —Stacy (Mom of 1)

It's Not All About the Crying

Towards the end of the second month, things are hopefully falling into place—you and your baby are hitting your stride. The 7:00 p.m. going-to-sleep-process is smoother (though it's entirely possible that it's still challenging). The top-up bottle is adding the extra calories needed to power your little one through extra hours of sleep. You've hopefully dropped one, maybe even two feedings. And you've stretched out the longest sleep period to anywhere from 4 to 8 hours.

All of this is baby-led. You're doing a lot of things we've talked about throughout the book to set your baby up for success, but for the most part, any progress has been spurred by the smallest member of your family.

Regardless of where you are in the process, you should be starting to see that introducing top-up bottles and dream feeds is working at extending sleep. Hopefully, by now you've also started to recognize that it's not letting your baby cry that's helping you make progress. We've mentioned a few times that it's okay to not rush in every time your baby makes a little fuss. But we also haven't explicitly told you to let your baby cry on and on in an effort to teach self-soothing. It's probably time for a little reminder that the Dream Feed Method doesn't require crying in order to be successful.

We mention this now because we find that this is about the time when parents who are doing great with the Dream Feed Method also become inundated with information from other parents, books, and blogs. These sources will preach, among many things, the importance of self-soothing. And for a baby to learn how to self-soothe, he must also be given a chance to try it out, which often involves a little bit of crying. Because the Dream Feed Method involves so little crying, some parents may start to worry that their baby will not learn how to self-soothe.

So, here's the explicit guidance we have to offer you for this phase: If you made it to 3-hour scheduled feedings at the very minimum, you don't ever need to listen to your baby cry for his meal. But nor do we think there is anything particularly wrong with letting your baby cry for a few minutes. You'll likely still have plenty of opportunities to experience this outside of mealtimes. And when you do have one of those magical little moments where your baby wakes briefly in the night, cries for two minutes, but then gets himself comfortable and goes back to sleep, it will feel pretty awesome.

However, what we find is that some parents, bombarded with too much conflicting guidance, become overly concerned with the question of crying. All we're trying to say in this chapter is that you don't need to worry about it. If you're reading this, and your baby is less than three months old, *and* you've been making progress with the Dream Feed Method, then whether your baby cries occasionally or not won't make a difference at all. Let the people who start sleep training in month five preach about self-soothing. You're not going to need it.

Now, a couple of caveats. If you've not yet successfully made it to a 3-hour schedule, it is likely that your baby is doing too much snacking and needs to learn how to last the 3 hours. And there may be some tears involved to get there. We would encourage you to go back to the chapter on 3-hour schedules until you are able to successfully get your baby to take larger meals and go 3 hours between feedings.

The second caveat is that if you are past four months, then you're effectively off the Dream Feed Method schedule. Your baby has likely learned some associations that now have to be unlearned—and that almost always involves tears.

Your Baby Will Start Feeding a Lot

One of the things we often see with parents who have early success with the Dream Feed Method is that their babies start to feed a lot more at night, either from the breast or from the bottle or from both. That itself is a good thing. It means that the baby is learning to take a larger feeding in preparation for a longer night's sleep.

In general, if the baby feeds more, he'll sleep longer. And because the rest of the day is generally split up into about 3-hour periods between feedings, having one period of the day that goes much longer between feedings necessitates that the feeding right before it will, on average, be bigger. Some moms find this surprising and even concerning.

If you know that your baby takes about four ounces a feeding throughout the day and then gobbles down six ounces at night, you may start to wonder what constitutes too much. And if you start comparing notes with other moms or, dare we mention, check the Internet, you may find that your baby's nighttime feeding is larger than many other babies. This easily leads to second-guessing.

Let us assuage those fears. You (almost) can't overfeed your baby at night. We'll address the "almost" part of that sentence in a second. But, to be clear, the further away you get from small snacks that only last a couple of hours into a single, much larger feeding that can last the entire night, the better.

Most of sleep training, regardless of what method you use, is simply teaching your baby to take a larger feeding and last longer with it. So, by all means give your baby as much sustenance as he'll take. And what we've uncovered with top-up bottles is that babies are capable of taking in more milk than their mother may be able to provide in a single feeding.

Your goal with every top-up bottle or dream feed replacement bottle is to feed your baby as much as he wants and to end with a little bit left in the bottle when he indicates to you that he is done. Conversely, if the bottle is empty at the end of the feeding, then you probably started off without enough in the bottle. Early on, a baby will indicate that he's done feeding by simply falling asleep. In the second and third month (typically after you've introduced dream feeds), he'll learn how to purse his lips, stick out his tongue, or turn away to indicate that he no longer wants a bottle in his mouth.

One additional note: there is no concern that feeding him as much as he wants now will lead to an obese baby. The nutrition you're providing him, as well as the extra sleep that he is achieving as a result, is positively contributing to his brain development.

Breast milk and the formulas designed to supplement it are the absolute most nutritious food he'll ever have in his life. Give him every drop that he wants so that the intense process of building his body and developing his brain has as much fuel as it needs. And, as an important side effect, he'll also sleep longer.

Paced Bottle Feeding

As soon as your baby starts taking more than an ounce in either the top-up bottle or in the dream feed, it's time to be cognizant of the speed with which he's feeding. Even the smallest sized bottle nipple will release the milk at a faster flow than breastfeeding.

In the middle of the night, that faster flow of milk can be beneficial in giving your baby a full feeding in half the time. Just make sure you're doing it in a way that's not causing any discomfort to your baby.

If you're feeding your baby and he takes the bottle naturally, you get a good burp out, and he goes down just fine, then all is well. Continue what you're doing. If you see signs that you've fed him too quickly, then you need to slow down the bottle-feeding.

The two biggest signs of this are excessive spitting up and gas pains. Excessive spitting up you'll know immediately. Don't mistake it for your baby being overfed. It's more likely that your baby was fed too quickly. To slow down the feeding process, pause between ounces and give your baby more time to settle and digest. It's not uncommon to do a full burping between each ounce.

Top-up bottles and dream feed bottles do give your baby more milk than they otherwise would have gotten without them, and more milk than they're accustomed to in other feedings. Those are both really good things. You want your baby taking a larger than average feeding before he sleeps for a longer than average period of time. That's the whole point of what we're doing.

Pacing the bottle feeding and adding extra burping makes it possible for him to learn to accept more milk, and thus sleep longer before feeling hungry.

If you notice that your baby is gassy after the feeding and struggles to go down because of it, try to get a sense of whether this gassiness is similar or different than after non-bottle feedings. If your baby's in general just gassy (even during non-bottle feeds), then he's just in a gassy period and will soon outgrow it. This is typical, especially in the first two months. While there are several things you can do about that, the most important is simply to wait until the gassy period has finished. For most babies this happens sometime in the second month. But if your baby is significantly gassier after a bottle-supported feeding, then a slower feeding period and more burps along the way will help significantly. Also, refer **Page 110** of this book for more tips on how to navigate gas pains.

Reviewing the Initial Schedule

So, how does this all come together? In case it's helpful, we'll next describe a very specific plan that works for a lot of couples.

7:00 p.m.

Mom prepares the baby for bed, changing the diaper, swaddling, and getting the room ready for sleep-time (white noise machine, low lights, etc.). She then gets comfortable and breastfeeds the baby from both sides.

7:20 p.m.

Dad slips in with two warm top-up bottles in hand. One bottle has the bare minimum breast milk and the other bottle has warm formula in case your baby wants more than you predict. Together, Mom and Dad seamlessly transition the baby from breast to Dad's arms, where he gives the top-up bottles. Mom leaves and takes the next few hours off.

7:30 p.m. to 10:00 p.m.

Dad does his best to get the baby down. In theory, Dad leaves the baby in his crib while the baby is drowsy but still awake, and the baby puts himself to sleep. But more often, this will take some hard work. Once the baby is asleep, Dad goes to sleep.

10:00 p.m. (or whenever the baby wakes up)

Mom, you're on. You breastfeed from both sides. Burp and change (if absolutely necessary) and get the baby back down.

1:00 a.m. (or whenever the baby wakes up)

Mom, this one's yours, too. Again you'll breastfeed from both sides and change his diaper, if needed, before getting the baby back down.

4:00 a.m.

This will be the dream feed, which means, Dad, you'll set an alarm for this feeding. Once again, prepare two bottles, one with a bare minimum of expressed breast milk and another with formula as a buffer. These two separate bottles ensure you don't waste a drop of breast milk (or liquid gold, as we've heard some moms call it) and still ensure your baby gets as much as he wants. You'll give the dream feed at exactly 4:00 a.m., doing everything you can to have the baby not wake up. No changing and no lights on.

6:30 a.m.

Dad, this is your time to shine. You're in charge of placating your baby until that 7:00 a.m. feed.

7:00 a.m.

Mom feeds from the breast. Because you skipped a feeding, your breasts should be tremendously full of milk, likely leaving extra after your baby has gotten her fill. Pump afterward and store that excess milk for later top-up bottles.

That's the typical routine for most parents when they're still at three night-time feedings. Notice a couple of things about this routine: Dad gets one good chunk of sleep from approximately 8:00 p.m. or 9:00 p.m. (whenever the baby goes down) until 4:00 a.m., and then another chunk of sleep from about 4:30 a.m. to 6:30 a.m. Mom gets to take a couple of hours off following the 7:00 p.m. feeding until the 10:00 p.m. feeding and can either rest or relax, before getting a longer period of sleep from about 1:30 a.m. until 7:00 a.m.

For both parents, this phase of the Dream Feed Method is undoubtedly hard work, but it's also doable. The decision to use one replacement bottle, which Dad is empowered to give, has a dramatic effect on how much sleep Mom gets. Some nights it will seem that this schedule is far too regimented for the reality of what your baby is doing. That's fine. Don't expect any semblance of consistency at first. But after a few days or possibly weeks, we bet you'll find that your nightly schedule mirrors this quite closely. Yes, there will be times when the schedule breaks down due to off-kilter feedings, gassiness, or fussiness. But if you can get into this routine sometime within in the first month of The Dream Feed Method, consider it a huge success.

4. Feed a Little Earlier Each Night: Weeks Six Through Sixteen

Goals:

✓ **Feed a littler earlier and hold off until 7:00 a.m.**

✓ **Stretch the longest sleep to 6 hours and drop the first feeding, and then...**

✓ **...Stretch the longest sleep to 9 hours and drop second feeding, and then...**

✓ **...Stretch the longest sleep to 12 hours and drop the final feeding**

(This is go time, parents. You can do this!!!)

Feed a Little Earlier Each Night

Once you've found your rhythm with the dream feeds, it's time to start feeding a little earlier each night and stretching your baby's longest sleep duration.

To review, you're currently starting feeds at 7:00 p.m., 10:00 p.m., 1:00 a.m., 4:00 a.m., and then 7:00 a.m. That breaks the night into four distinct 3-hour sleeping periods.

(Okay, we know that in actuality your baby is not a robot and so your feeding times might not look identical to these. But you're savvy by now, Dream Feed Method parents, so you understand the basic structure.)

Your first step is only going to be moving your 4:00 a.m. feeding back to 3:45 a.m. with a dream feed. Now your baby has a full belly, is swaddled tightly, and is ready to sleep. You already know your baby is accustomed to going 3 hours until the 7:00 a.m. feeding. By moving his dream feed back by 15 minutes, you will find on the first morning that he wakes up exactly 3 hours later at 6:45 a.m.

Now, you just have to hold him off from feeding until 7:00 a.m. You can rock him, sing to him, or bounce him. You can use a pacifier or a vibrating swing. You just have to soothe him for 15 minutes without feeding him.

Your baby will adjust quickly. When you successfully reach 7:00 a.m. three days in a row without too much struggle, the ratchet is set. Your baby has now proven he can go from 3:45 a.m. to 7:00 a.m. Now you move that dream feed back another 15 minutes to 3:30 a.m. Following this, he'll probably wake up at about 6:45 a.m. again because he's used to 3 hours and 15 minutes of sleep. And again, you'll need to hold him off for 15 minutes. And again, he'll adjust. Now you've established 3:30 a.m. to 7:00 a.m. as his new longest sleep duration. You've stretched backward from 3 hours to 3.5 hours.

And remember, you don't just move that 4:00 a.m. feeding to 3:30 a.m., you move all the feedings back at the same time. Feedings now start at 7:00 p.m., 9:30 p.m., 12:30 a.m., 3:30 a.m., and 7:00 a.m.

You'll notice that the first sleep period of the night is shorter. It used to be 3 hours, from 7:00 p.m. to 10:00 p.m., but now you're providing a dream feed earlier than he needs it! Your baby could last longer, but you're purposefully shortening this first sleep period in order to pull the rest of the night backward. As you continue to move the dream feeds backward, the period after this first feeding will continue to be shortened.

At this point, you're putting your baby down at 7:00 p.m. and then offering a dream feed just 1.5 hours later. When he's not yet hungry enough for a full feeding, you're ready to drop the first feeding altogether.

You're going to be feeding at 7:00 p.m., 10:00 p.m., 1:00 a.m., and 7:00 a.m. Your baby's longest sleep period will extend to 6 hours.

Your baby isn't actually going to make it all 6 hours on the first night, from 1:00 a.m. to 7:00 a.m. But he'll get close. And either you'll start that 7:00 a.m. feeding a little bit earlier or you'll hold him off a little bit longer. And, remember, you don't ever have to let him cry that entire time. You can rock him, bounce him, put him in the vibrating chair—anything to help him get closer to feeding at 7:00 a.m. He will adjust in a few days.

Here again is the entire backward stretching schedule.

Figure 3. Backward Stretching Schedule

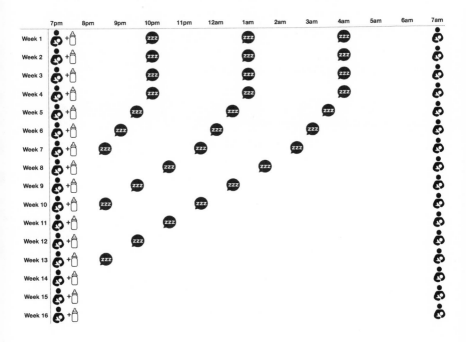

Feeding plus a Top-Up Bottle

Normal feeding when baby awakes (breast and/or bottle)

Dream Feed (breast and/or bottle)

The Meet-in-the-Middle Schedule

So far, we've recommended that you preempt each nighttime awakening and stretch the sleep durations backward. Now that you understand how it works, we'll next introduce a variation that works just as well. Instead of stretching backwards, you'll meet in the middle.

You'll still start somewhere towards the end of the first month or beginning of the second month with the same 3-hour schedule: 7:00 p.m., 10:00 p.m., 1:00 a.m., 4:00 a.m., and 7:00 a.m.

You'll also still move that 4:00 a.m. feeding backward in small intervals, starting from 4:00 a.m. to 3:45 a.m. And again, you'll hold off your baby until the 7:00 a.m. feeding. That means this final sleep period will stretch from 3 hours to 3.5 hours, and so on.

So far, everything's the same.

Now, instead of moving the other nighttime feedings back by the same small interval, you'll let your baby sleep as long as she wants to start the night. You'll let her naturally stretch forward the first half of the night. If she naturally extends 15 minutes to 10:15 p.m.—great. Now your night looks like this:

- Feeding and top-up at 7:00 p.m.

- Naturally wake at 10:15 p.m., followed by feeding.

- Naturally wake at 1:15 a.m., followed by feeding.

- Scheduled dream feed at 3:45 a.m.

- Hold off until 7:00 a.m. feeding.

You don't actually do anything to stretch your baby forward at the beginning of the night. However, once she shows that she can go a certain amount of time, you set that as the new benchmark. For example, you now know your baby can go from 7:00 p.m. to 10:15 p.m. However, the next night she wakes up ready to feed at 10:05 p.m. You'll now actively hold her off for 10 minutes to get back to her previous best.

As you can see, the middle sleep periods are starting to compress. Instead of compressing the first sleeping period of the night, you're compressing either the second or third sleep period (doesn't matter which) until it's eventually time to drop one of them.

The benefits of this schedule are that you get to let your baby sleep as long as she wants in one direction, while doing the disciplined method of stretching backward at the end of the night. This can also make more intuitive sense for some parents who struggle with the concept of meddling with a peacefully sleeping baby.

The challenge is that navigating the exact timing of middle-of-the-night feedings can be a little difficult. You and your partner have to be on the same page. You have to be really in tune with how your baby is doing.

Here's how a full Meet-in-the-Middle Schedule could look:

Figure 4. Meet-in-the-Middle Schedule

	7pm	8pm	9pm	10pm	11pm	12am	1am	2am	3am	4am	5am	6am	7am
Week 1	● + 🍼			●			●			zzz			●
Week 2	● + 🍼			●			●			zzz			●
Week 3	● + 🍼			●			●			zzz			●
Week 4	● + 🍼			●			●			zzz			●
Week 5	● + 🍼				●			●		zzz			●
Week 6	● + 🍼					●			zzz				●
Week 7	● + 🍼					●		zzz					●
Week 8	● + 🍼						●	zzz					●
Week 9	● + 🍼					zzz							●
Week 10	● + 🍼				zzz								●
Week 11	● + 🍼			zzz									●
Week 12	● + 🍼		zzz										●
Week 13	● + 🍼	zzz											●
Week 14	● + 🍼												●
Week 15	● + 🍼												●
Week 16	● + 🍼												●

● + 🍼   Feeding plus a Top-Up Bottle

●   Normal feeding when baby awakes (breast and/or bottle)

zzz   Dream Feed (breast and/or bottle)

A couple more observations:

This schedule still culminates in the same way: one feed stretches all the way backward to 8:30 p.m. before being dropped altogether.

In the middle section, weeks five to ten, this schedule can get a little dicey as you drop from three feedings to two feedings to one feeding. It happens a little bit faster in this schedule, which can be a good thing, but dropping each feeding often involves a challenging transition.

But once you get down to a single nighttime feeding, you'll feel like you're winning. You're actually only halfway done with extending your baby's sleep to 12 full hours, but it will feel much closer because you're only getting up once per night. And if you're effectively splitting the responsibility with your partner, then you will actually have some nights with no feedings at all!

So, which to choose? Try whichever feels right. If it doesn't work, try the other. It really depends on what you and your partner find intuitive, and it will depend on the baby in some cases. If yours is naturally a long-stretch sleeper, and she's showing that she can and wants to sleep later and later past that 10:00 p.m. feeding, this might be the option for you.

Dropping the First Feeding When Following the Meet-in-the-Middle Schedule

Now let's talk about dropping the first feeding. To review:

- Mom does 7:00 p.m. breastfeeding.

- Dad does 7:00 p.m. top-up bottle, following the breastfeed.

- Mom does 10:00 p.m. breastfeeding.

- Mom does 1:00 a.m. breastfeeding.

- Dad does 4:00 a.m. scheduled dream feed bottle.

- Dad holds off until Mom starts 7:00 a.m. breastfeeding.

The 10:00 p.m. and the 1:00 a.m. feeding are going to naturally drift later into the night. It doesn't matter by how much, and you don't have to force it or do any holding off. You're just going to let your baby lead the way. But the roles for Mom and Dad will stay the same. So, you may notice that your baby is sleeping until 10:30 p.m. instead of 10:00 p.m. That's fine. Mom feeds at 10:30 p.m., which pushes the 1:00 a.m. feeding to 1:30 a.m. or even 2:00 a.m. That's fine as well; Mom is still in charge of that feeding.

Or your baby may choose to stay locked in at about 10:00 p.m. on the first feeding, but will sleep longer until the second feeding. In this scenario, there will be a feeding around 10:00 p.m. and then the second feeding around 1:30 a.m. or 2:00 a.m. Your baby will also surprise you at some point with a big jump when he goes from the 7:00 p.m. feeding all the way until, say, 12:30 a.m.

Mom, you'll enjoy this period because you're getting to see your baby sleep soundly as long as he wants, and you'll be so proud of him every time he sleeps a little bit longer. You also don't have any holding off to do. When your baby wakes up, as long as it's been more than 3 hours, you just feed him.

Dad, your role is different. You're in charge of that 4:00 a.m. dream feed as well as holding off the baby from whenever he wakes up around 6:30 a.m. until the 7:00 a.m. breastfeeding. The timing of these two feedings is driven by you, not the baby. You're going to shift that 4:00 a.m. feeding, which is a dream feed, a little bit earlier each night.

The first step is offering that feeding at 3:45 a.m., no matter when the last feeding was. And, as you're well familiar by now, you'll hold the baby off until 7:00 a.m. the next morning, regardless of when he wakes.

It may take a couple of days for your baby to adjust, but as soon as he's successful at waiting until the 7:00 a.m. feed, you'll shift the dream feed backwards another 15 minutes. Now, you'll be trying to help him last from the 3:30 a.m. feeding until 7:00 a.m.

During this period, Mom is letting her two feedings drift forward, and Dad is pulling his dream feeding backward. At some point in the first few weeks of doing this, your feedings will collide and you'll be ready to drop one of Mom's feedings.

The scenario might look something like this: your baby has naturally started going from 7:00 p.m. until let's say 11:00 p.m., and then 11:00 p.m. until maybe 2:30 a.m. Dad has pulled his dream feed backward to 3:15 a.m., and so you've found that the baby is barely hungry for it, since he's breast fed only 45 minutes before. Maybe you're only giving him an ounce or so before he communicates that he's not hungry. This is when you know it is time to drop Mom's final breastfeed of the night.

Now, Mom covers the first feeding, which is somewhere between 10:00 p.m. and as late as 1:00 a.m., and Dad covers the second feeding, which is as early as 2:00 a.m. or as late as 3:30 a.m. And Dad still has the responsibility for holding the baby off until 7:00 a.m. Now, you've made the huge, awesome, incredibly relieving jump from three feedings to two feedings.

As we mentioned, you're still some ways out from achieving 12 hours of sleep, but already you'll find your nights start to feel significantly easier. Mom, between about 7:20 p.m. and whenever the baby wakes up for his first feed, you'll get some time to relax or even catch a few hours of sleep. After that first feeding, you're off the rest of the night. You'll be able to get a decent 2 to 4 hours sleep in the first half of the night followed by a nice 4 to 5 hours in the second half.

Dad, you're responsible for the 7:00 p.m. top-up bottle and getting the baby down for the night. Then, you will get to sleep a solid handful of hours before your alarm goes off for that dream feed sometime around 3:00 a.m.

This period of two feedings a night will feel significantly easier than three feedings a night, but it is still hard work. Sleep for both parents is still disjointed, but hopefully you've also found a rhythm. You both understand your roles, and you've become accustomed to what it takes to feed and get the baby down.

You're in the thick of it at this point, but remember, this is the time to not give up hope. For many of you, you're just a few short weeks from dropping another feeding and achieving sustainable sleep.

Dropping the Second Feeding

To review, mom will be doing the 7:00 p.m. breastfeeding followed by dad with the top-up bottle before getting the baby down for the night. Mom takes the next feeding whenever the baby lets you know it's time (sometime between 10:00 p.m. and 1:00 a.m.). Dad, you're giving the dream feed between 2:00 a.m. and 3:30 a.m. and then holding the baby off between 6:30 a.m. and 7:00 a.m., when Mom begins the day by breastfeeding.

The dream feed will continue to inch backwards in 15-minute increments just like you've done since the beginning, when you started at 4:00 a.m. By now it has reached 2:00 a.m., and your baby is sleeping a solid 5-hour stretch before he's awake and ready for the 7:00 a.m. feeding.

Soon your 10:00 p.m. to 1:00 a.m. feeding and your approximately 2:00 a.m. feeding are going to start to meet in the middle. You'll find that your baby is barely hungry for the 2:00 a.m. dream feed, as he was just recently fed by Mom an hour or so before. Now you're ready to drop one of those feedings, and it will be Mom's. Dad will take it over with a dream feed. To achieve this, you'll let your baby sleep as long as he can go, and then Dad will offer a bottle that will power him all the way until morning. The first few mornings as you transition you may be getting up early at 6:00 a.m. or 6:30 a.m., which means you'll need to hold him off for a longer period. But very soon, he'll adjust.

Mom, this stage has a totally obvious implication—because you're not feeding halfway through the night, your breasts will become engorged, probably making it difficult to sleep. You'll have two options: either take over the feeding from your partner, or wake up and pump, while Dad maintains the dream feed. For some moms, it can feel strange to be pumping while Dad feeds a bottle. But, as we've noted several times, there are advantages in terms of the efficiency that bottle-feeding provides. Either way, do what you feel works best.

Dad, at this point you should be feeling great for two reasons. First, you're only getting up once in the middle of the night, book-ended by two reasonably long periods of sleep. Second, you have given Mom something almost no new moms get this early. She has the night off from around 7:20 p.m. until 7:00 a.m. Not to downplay the responsibility of middle-of-the-night pumping, but, relatively speaking, she'll likely feel like a million bucks at this point.

This is when it all starts to come together. Mom will be regaining her energy, you'll both be finding your stride as parents, and your baby will probably be entering a new, more contented phase as those relentless gas pains begin to subside.

So, if you've made it to this stage of just one feeding a night, you will actually find that while the hard work is not complete, the overall happiness in your household will have improved dramatically. Your new struggle will be holding your tongue when talking to friends who are still stuck with both a late-night feeding around 11:00 p.m. plus another feeding around 4:00 a.m. (Don't brag; just give them your copy of this book as a gift.)

You're now on to the final stage of the Dream Feed Method.

Dropping the Last Feeding

Dad, you know the drill. Your middle of the night dream feeding shifts 15 minutes earlier, holding steady just until your baby can easily last until 7:00 a.m., when you'll once again shift that dream feed. You should be able to make about an hour of progress a week. Soon that 2 a.m. feeding is pulled backward to 1:00 a.m., midnight, and finally you're down to a single feeding at 11:00 p.m., when you'll find it's just as easy to simply stay up for it.

Keep pulling it back earlier and earlier, and soon you'll be giving the dream feed at 10:00 p.m. Your baby is sleeping a total of 9 straight hours. As you move back even closer to the 7:00 p.m. feeding, you'll find that your baby doesn't need as much milk since he's been recently given a full feed by breast as well as a top-up bottle. The quantity that your baby takes in that 9:30 p.m. to 10:00 p.m. feeding will naturally start to reduce.

Dropping this dream feed can happen in one of two ways. Some parents will choose to simply reduce the bottle amount gradually until it's virtually nonexistent, while others will continue to pull the feeding backward even earlier. Once your baby doesn't need that feeding, he'll just let it go.

Many parents tell us this milestone sneaks up on them—suddenly your baby will be going from his 7:00 p.m. feeding until 7:00 a.m. the next morning. It will seem almost anti-climactic.

Your new, and more permanent, routine will keep a few of the core elements you're now used to. Dad, you might continue giving the top-up bottle and being responsible for getting the baby down for the night. Mom, you'll do the 7:00 p.m. breastfeed, and you'll wake up when you want to pump in the middle of the night.

Your Goal Is Dusk till Dawn

Around this time, you may be losing steam. You've made real progress, but the Holy Grail of 12 hours still feels out of reach. You may be tempted to settle for less.

Keep going! You can do this. Those last few hours matter.

Babies are capable of and benefit immensely from sleeping from dusk till dawn. That's what *we* consider a "full night's sleep," 12 hours without any parental intervention—no soothing, no feeding.

For your infant, getting to 12 hours will absolutely affect his overall mood. You will notice it immediately. Your baby will be less fussy than the other babies in his playgroup. You will be told how lucky you are to have such an "easy baby," but the reality is that he's simply well rested (as are you). This is what results from your perseverance toward teaching your baby to sleep those few extra hours per night.

The power of setting your goal of 12 full hours also forces you to push through two particularly tough nighttime ruts that you would much rather avoid.

The most brutal of these nighttime ruts is the 5:00 a.m. wake up. Many parents consider 5:00 a.m. to be the start of their day (*every day*) because that's when their baby wakes up. We believe there's simply no need for this to be the case. Babies should be able to sleep until 7:00 a.m., and when they do wake up before 7:00 a.m., they should be content in their crib until 7:00 a.m.

Those 2 extra hours of sleep are priceless—yes, for your baby and his rapidly developing brain, but maybe even more so for you. Either you get those hours of sleep for yourself as well, or you can get up early and do any morning activity you want: a leisurely breakfast, or 45 minutes at the gym, or simply having the uninterrupted time to get yourself ready for the day.

The other typical nighttime rut is the infamous bedtime battle. So many parents become accustomed to a bedtime routine that might begin at 7:00 p.m., but doesn't actually end until around 10:00 p.m., when the baby finally calls it quits and falls asleep. Here, too, the baby loses out on 3 important hours of sleep, and, equally important, both parents have lost out on an evening to themselves.

A consistent (and successful) 7:00 p.m. bedtime opens up a world of possibilities—what will you do with those 2, 3, maybe 4 hours a night before you turn in? It also makes hiring babysitters that much easier. Need we say more?

All of these incredible positives come because you persisted with sleep training beyond what most people might consider "through the night."

A Researcher's Perspective: Five Hour Blocks of Sleep Are Not Enough

You will find conflicting advice in the literature about what it actually means. There are many who recommend that a single five-hour block of sleep overnight can be safely assessed as "sleeping through the night."

This is incorrect.

While we as adults are somewhat fatigue resistant, for young children, this is not true. For an infant to function at their behavioral best during the hours of daylight, they need approximately 12 hours of sleep at night.

When children are even one sleep cycle short of this suggested overnight sleep duration, their behavior will be adversely affected. While the child may have missed less than 10% of their overnight sleep, the negative impact upon the following day is more like 30 to 40%.

The negative effect will appear all day but particularly after approximately 4:00 p.m. If your baby is "high maintenance" between 4:00 p.m and 5:00 p.m., then it's likely the baby was short of sleep in the previous 24-hour period.

If your baby gets into this late afternoon period and maintains a stable disposition, eats well, and achieves their nighttime sleep efficiently, the total sleep which you have achieved in the previous 24 hours is approximately correct.

—Brian Symon, M.D.

Troubleshooting the 11:00 p.m. and 4:00 a.m. Feeding Pattern

Let's say you are currently doing feedings at 11:00 p.m. and 4:00 a.m. That's two times a parent needs to adjust their sleep for a feeding. Wouldn't it be nicer if you only had to interrupt your sleep for one feeding?

Try this:

Introduce a 9:30 p.m. dream feed and a 2:30 a.m. dream feed. By introducing a dream feed at 9:30 p.m., a full 90 minutes before he usually wakes up from his first stretch of sleep, you're allowing one parent to do the feeding before going to sleep for the rest of the night. The other parent can go to sleep early and be responsible for the 2:30 a.m. feeding.

If your baby takes a 9:30 p.m. dream feed, he won't accept the full feeding, either by breast or by bottle, because his stomach is not 100 percent empty. But he'll still take something, maybe 50 to 75 percent of a full feeding. That, in addition to the milk that's still in his belly, should take him about the same length of time he was previously making. So, if he was previously going from 11:00 p.m. till 4:00 a.m., a five-hour stretch, now he'll go from 9:30 p.m. to 2:30 a.m., the same five-hour stretch.

At 2:30 a.m., he should either be just waking up, ready to wake up soon, or sleeping soundly. Regardless, you're going to feed him at 2:30 a.m. because you know he can go another four-hour stretch and you're trying to feed him before he wakes up completely. Your hope is that he takes a full dream feeding, goes down easily, and lasts to 7:00 a.m. He may sleep lighter (that's code for fussing loudly) in that 6:00 a.m. to 7:00 a.m. period, but he should be able to either console himself or be consoled without a feeding.

This trick, introducing an earlier dream feed, should work immediately, and there's very little risk in trying it. The biggest risk is you feed him at 9:30 p.m., he isn't able to take a big enough feeding to last his normal 5 hours, and he needs something much earlier than 2:30 a.m. This means he's up far before 7:00 a.m., and you're stuck consoling him at, say, 5:00 a.m. or 5:30 a.m.

If this happens the first night, try at least once more using bottle-feeding for the dream feeds. Bottle-feeding with either expressed breast milk or formula often gives just enough extra milk to add almost an hour to each stretch of sleeping, which is enough to get him back to the 7:00 a.m. goal more easily. If that still doesn't work, then dropping back to the 9:30 p.m. dream feed was too aggressive, and you should take a smaller step. The next night, try 10:00 p.m., which should get him to 3:00 a.m.

It may take you three or four nights to find the right time for the first dream feed and to get the quantity of milk accepted in each dream feed through the breast, bottle, or a combination of both, but most parents can successfully introduce this dream feed and establish a new routine.

Now, one parent stays up "late" (9:30 p.m.) for the first dream feed, and the other is handling the second dream feed. Then, the first parent is responsible for consoling him in the morning as needed. That's a great pattern for a couple to be in.

And best of all, you're now well set-up to stretch out the feedings.

Introduce his first dream feed 15 minutes earlier per night, initially that will be at 9:15 p.m. In lockstep, offer the second dream feed 15 minutes earlier as well, at 2:15 a.m. Every time he makes it to 7:00 a.m. without wailing, you call it a success. He may wake up and fuss on his own. He may wake up and need light consoling. Either way, you have achieved your goal, and you move back each dream feed by an additional 15 minutes the next night.

If he wakes up early, say before 6:00 a.m., and needs significant consoling, or requires an earlier feeding, then you hold steady until he proves to you that he's adjusted to the new schedule. Your goal is to make about an hour's worth of progress per week. Soon that first dream feed will be getting close to 8:30 p.m., and with his belly still mostly full, he'll be taking a very small additional dream feed.

If he's still maintaining his 5-hour middle stretch of sleep, he'll be making it until 1:30 a.m. for his next dream feed. You've successfully stretched the final period of sleep to 5.5 hours, from 1:30 a.m. until 7:00 a.m.

Now, he's going to allow you to easily drop that 8:30 p.m. feeding.

Be ready to feed him anywhere from 12:30 a.m. to 1:00 a.m., and if that happens, also be prepared for him to need some extra consoling from 6:00 a.m. to 7:00 a.m. while he adjusts to the new schedule.

You may endure a couple of difficult nights during this specific transition, but most babies can make the leap. And once your baby does, you've successfully made it to only one middle-of-the-night feeding! Congrats!

Now you know what to do: offer that 1:30 a.m. feeding as a dream feed about fifteen minutes earlier each night, aiming for one hour of progress per week.

As far as expectations go, progressing from two feedings at 11:00 p.m. and 4:00 a.m. to a single 1:00 a.m. feeding is LIFE-CHANGING for parents. The transition can be done in literally one week with almost no crying. And from the onset, at least one parent gets most of the night off!

Just When You Thought Things Were Going Well

From time to time your baby may have random bouts of waking in the middle of the night.

Let's say you've reached the point where you're accustomed to your baby sleeping 9+ hours, and you're making that final push to stretch it toward a full 12 hours. All of a sudden, your baby starts waking up at 4:00 a.m. once again. That nine-hour stretch wasn't as locked-in as you thought.

Now, your baby has already proven to herself and to you that she can sleep 9 hours without needing a feeding, so she doesn't "need" to be fed when she has just awakened unexpectedly at 4:00 a.m.

This is a soothing problem, not a hunger problem.

Although a quick feeding at 4:00 a.m. will get that baby to go right back to sleep, it will have consequences. You might be able to do that once without too much impact, but we've observed that the more common scenario is that 4:00 a.m. feed creates an instant pattern. Get ready, because you're then in for a 4:00 a.m. wake-up call the next night, too. And the next. And the one after that. Just like that, you will see all of your independent sleep progress wither away into a newly established habit of waking at 4:00 a.m.

So, instead of offering a 4:00 a.m. feeding when you know your baby doesn't need it, just help your baby go back to sleep. Sounds easy enough, right? But we know that at 4:00 a.m., *nothing* feels easy. The challenge is that you'll need to help your baby learn to fall back to sleep without the soothing accompaniment of milk.

After coaching many moms through this, we've recognized that the act of removing your baby from the crib to soothe him, while better than offering a bottle, also introduces another habit that is hard to break. Just as your baby would get used to a 4:00 a.m. feed, so too would she get used to a 4:00 a.m. cuddle; and she'll easily confuse it with "time to get up for the day." Our recommendation is to sit down next to the crib. Put your arm lightly on your baby's chest and hold the pacifier in his mouth. In an ideal world, you can do this for five to ten minutes and then leave. Your baby will either already be asleep or will put himself back to sleep.

But let's consider the non-ideal scenario for a second. Let's just say it seems like your baby is inconsolable unless you are physically there, putting your arm on her chest and holding that pacifier in her mouth. It's 4:00 a.m., and all you want to do is go back to sleep.

Dig in deep and prepare to sit there, even for as long as an hour. If you don't remove the baby from the crib, don't turn on the lights, and don't provide a feeding, the random 4:00 a.m. waking won't continue. The only thing that will really mess this up is if you decide to give in with a feed or a cuddle. It'll be a band-aid, and one that you'll need to pull out the next night, and all of the ones following it.

The other alternative is to let your baby cry himself back to sleep. Remember, you've already proven that he doesn't need the extra feeding, so you're not starving your baby. We know how much you hate hearing your baby cry, but you *can* decide to simply close the door and let your baby cry himself back to sleep. The crying is not going to last for hours.

This will be nowhere near cry-it-out levels. But, if every once in a while you experience a random wake-up, and your baby cries for a few minutes before putting herself back to sleep, it's completely normal. While you've done the hard work of helping her go a full night without eating, she will still occasionally wake for other reasons. No psychological harm will be imprinted on your baby; in fact, the crying will be harder on you than her (the first of so many of these moments). The good news is that this will pass fairly quickly, and when you make it to 12 hours of independent sleep by the fourth month, these random middle-of-the-night awakenings will become more and more rare, until they disappear completely.

A Researcher's Perspective: They'll Learn to Self-soothe

It takes time for your child to develop strength, coordination, balance, and confidence to "learn" to walk.

It takes time for your baby to develop night sleep consolidation, regular and long naps, and self-soothing skills to "learn" to sleep well.

> It comes as a surprise to many parents that healthy sleep habits do not develop automatically. In fact, parents can and do help or hinder the development of healthy sleep habits.
>
> —Marc Weissbluth, M.D., *Healthy Sleep Habits, Happy Child*

My Baby Keeps Waking Up at 6:00 a.m.

Many parents who are ultimately successful with the Dream Feed Method, getting their babies sleeping a full 12 hours from dusk till dawn by the end of the fourth month, become stuck early when their baby won't sleep past 6:00 a.m.

It's difficult to diagnose the exact issue here.

Sometimes dawn has started and a little bit of light is creeping into the room. That can be enough to wake up a baby. Sometimes there's sound in the house or apartment as people are getting up for the day. That can be enough to wake up a baby. Or even more common, they're just learning how to enter into that very last hour of semi-sleeplessness and aren't yet comfortable with lying in bed awake. This is part of the self-soothing that will naturally come along later.

Our general guidance is, if you can continue to make progress moving the final dream feed earlier and earlier, keep doing it even if you're only making it to 6:00 a.m. It's pretty common for a lot of babies to not make that very last hour of progress—successfully settling themselves from 6:00 a.m. to 7:00 a.m.—until the very end of the sleep training process.

Part 4:

Standard Sleep - Training Best Practices

Sleep when your baby sleeps.
Everyone knows this classic tip,
but I say why stop there?
Scream when your baby screams.
Take Benadryl when your baby takes Benadryl.
And walk around pantless when your
baby walks around pantless.

—Tina Fey

The Dream Feed Method is powerful but simple. And if you just follow its basic tenets, your baby will make huge gains in sleeping.

But that doesn't mean you should ignore other generally accepted sleep-training advice. What follows are best practices that originated in peer-reviewed research and have been proven again and again.

If you've already read other sleep-training books, you'll find much of this section familiar. Feel free to skim through it.

If you haven't read these other sources or are still debating what you will do, read through each section:

1. **Scheduled Feedings**

2. **Self-soothing**

3. **Low-stimulation Soothing**

4. **Crib vs. Room-sharing vs. Co-sleeping**

5. **A Dark, Loud Nursery**

6. **Problems and Solutions**

1. Scheduled Feedings

Without a good daytime feeding and napping schedule as a foundation, it's virtually impossible to have sleep-training success at night.

Sticking to a schedule during the day teaches your baby about predictability. It's the first time that he learns that he doesn't have to cry to get food. Food is simply going to come like it always has before. When you follow scheduled feedings from the very beginning, your baby simply grows up expecting it. However, when you start your baby with on-demand feedings, your baby grows up expecting immediate gratification instead.

Big problems occur when the on-demand provider decides it's no longer possible to keep it up and tries to establish a schedule several months in. You can imagine how difficult it is for a baby to understand why all of a sudden crying doesn't produce milk. And, thus, the instinct is to simply cry harder.

We follow the standard 3-hour cycle. Every cycle is measured by the beginning of the feeding, irrespective of when the feeding ends or when sleeping begins or when sleeping ends. Initially, begin the feedings at 7:00 a.m., 10 a.m., 1:00 p.m., 4:00 p.m., 7:00 p.m., 10:00 p.m., 1:00 a.m., and 4:00 a.m.

The pattern during the day is always: feed your baby, then have high-stimulation play time, and then go down for a nap. You probably won't be able to get to a firm schedule in the first couple of weeks, and that's okay. As long as you have established the schedule in the first month, you'll be in a great position for the rest of the Dream Feed Method.

Yes, there will be times, because you've chosen to follow a schedule, when you'll have to hold back from feeding your baby and will need to comfort her in other ways.

Scheduled feeding is also important for another, often overlooked reason— you as a parent can practice your sleep-soothing techniques during the day when you're more awake, rested, and patient.

When you set your scheduled feeding for 1:00 p.m. and your baby is hungry at 12:30 p.m., then you need to hold your baby off for 30 minutes to stay on schedule.

You'll use a bunch of tricks to get there: distracting with a pacifier or a toy, bobbing your baby on the knee, singing gently. These tricks are the same you need to use at night, but it's so much harder when you, yourself are half asleep. If anything, a good daytime sleep schedule trains the parent as much as it trains the baby.

Sleep Duration Is Just Time Between Feedings

A lot of parents get tripped up by thinking their baby's sleep should be a sound sleep. It's actually totally fine and completely normal for your baby to wake up a lot. Your baby will certainly be waking up every 45 minutes, because that's just how long his sleep cycle is.

So, don't create an unrealistic expectation that your baby will sleep soundly. When people say "sleep like a baby," they conjure up a notion of a pleasant, deep sleep.

In fact, "sleep like a baby" means a kicking, fussy, face-contorting struggle to learn this new skill. It will get easier for your baby later on, but for now, it is a struggle, especially during periods of gassiness when your baby's body is growing at such a tremendous rate.

Instead of focusing on whether your baby is soundly asleep the entire time, focus on the amount of time between feedings. That's actually what we are doing when we sleep train. We are lengthening the time between feedings and, accordingly, your baby's body has to learn to eat more before going to sleep so that he can go longer before his next meal.

Holding Off Until the Next Feeding

The whole philosophy of the Dream Feed Method is that you're giving your baby the opportunity to progress by just 10 to 15 minutes at a time. These small increments allow your baby's body time to adjust, take in more milk during feedings, and become accustomed to the feeling of having her stomach emptier toward the end of the sleep period. It's also done in small increments so that parents can prove to themselves that, if their baby wakes up in the middle of a scheduled sleep period, it doesn't mean he needs food.

For instance, if your baby has been consistently sleeping 4 hours or more during the final stretch of the night, and then one night you hear him crying halfway through that 4-hour stretch, you know it's not about food. She has already proven to you many times over that she can go those 4 hours. You know that she just woke up and is struggling to get back to sleep because this is a new skill.

You have three choices:

1. You can feed her, which will satiate her and put her back to sleep.
2. You can completely ignore the crying.
3. You can find other ways to soothe her and get her back to sleep.

If you pick option one, your baby would come to expect a feeding at that particular time every night. And the hope of sleeping dusk till dawn by the fourth month goes away.

You could also try option two, which follows the same philosophy as crying-it-out. It will work. However, the amount of trauma you will put on yourself, no matter how committed you are, will be significant. One of the benefits of the Dream Feed Method is that you don't have to consider that option.

Just take option number three—soothe your baby without feeding her. As long as you continue to maintain the time between feedings, even if you have to do an incredible amount of soothing work in between, your baby will learn to adjust.

2. Self-soothing

Babies don't sleep for a variety of reasons. If they're hungry, they don't sleep. If there's too much light, they don't sleep. If they're overtired, they don't sleep. If they're not used to sleeping, they don't sleep. If they feel uncomfortable, they don't sleep. And on, and on, and on.

Many parents get into a cycle of trying to correct for each of the things that is preventing good sleep as if elimination of enough of the issues will magically cause your baby to turn into a hearty sleeper. However, although elimination of these issues is necessary, it is not sufficient. Even in the most ideal setting, very few babies will magically develop into great sleepers, because sleeping for long periods has not yet been learned.

In the womb, your baby was able to sleep in 45-minute cycles independent of day or night. And for the first four or five weeks after birth, babies generally maintain that schedule, getting up to feed every 2 to 3 hours. So when you start moving toward a full night's sleep, it necessitates that your baby has to learn to deal with change.

And dealing with change is uncomfortable.

Babies, just like us, like stability. When you try to guide a baby from waking up every couple of hours to learning how to sleep 12 hours in a row, you are breaking an established cycle. And learning how to deal with something new and different is the act of self-soothing.

Even more important, self-soothing solves a lot of those symptoms many parents thought were keeping their kids up. A baby who knows how to self-soothe can last longer when they're a little hungry, can entertain themselves when they wake up before their parents do, and can put themselves back to sleep when they are awakened by a loud noise.

Self-soothing is an amazing skill. Without it, there's no real hope that they'll ever be able to sleep through the night.

Babies Wake Up Every 45 Minutes

In truth, 45 minutes is just how long a baby's sleep cycle is.

Adults, by the way, wake up every 90 minutes. You don't remember it most of the time, because you're so conditioned to going right back to sleep.

Babies wake up every 45 minutes, and at first they don't know how to put themselves back to sleep. First-time parents often don't know this and may assume that their baby is just a bad sleeper. Or they may assume that their baby is for some reason not comfortable enough to sleep, and thus needs more soothing, feeding, rocking, swaying, or singing. In reality, every baby, even if nothing is the matter, will wake up after 45 minutes and start crying.

The question is: how long does it take them to learn to fall back to sleep unassisted?

The entirety of the self-soothing research stems from this question. Since babies wake up regularly, those that take even just a few minutes to struggle by themselves to go back to sleep quickly learn how to do it. Those who don't have that opportunity to struggle for themselves for just a few minutes not only don't learn to do it, they latch on to this new association of waking up, crying, and always receiving external soothing.

Self-soothing Must Be Taught

For the first couple of weeks, you don't need to even think about self-soothing. Follow your instincts. Do everything your baby needs. It will feel right. Everything in your body will be telling you to protect this helpless little one whom you love so much.

After those first couple of weeks, habits start to be remembered. If your baby is used to being soothed immediately every time, that habit will become painful to break. You can teach self-soothing ever so gently, as long as you start early enough. And waiting until the fourth month is too late.

The goal of self-soothing is to teach a baby how to initially fall asleep and then fall back asleep on her own. If you actively resist introducing alternative ways of falling asleep, such as using props, rocking, or vibrating, your baby will start that much closer to the experience she'll have when she wakes up in the middle of the night. Every step you take that deviates from the behavior you'll want them to later have by themselves is one more act of removal your baby will fight against.

Researchers call these crutches *associations*. Associations are patterns that even a newborn can recognize. Going to sleep in a vibrating chair becomes an association, and the baby fails to learn that going to sleep can occur without the vibrating chair.

In addition to resisting the introduction of associations you'll have to remove later, you also need to allow your baby to struggle to soothe himself. This may sound absolutely ridiculous when we're talking about a baby less than a few months old, but the reality is that babies of all ages can learn how to soothe themselves. The only question is when to start.

Your four-week-old is crying in the middle of the night, and you've already ruled out hunger, diaper, loose swaddle, and gas. So, there's nothing wrong to fix. Your baby is just fussing to get back to sleep because she doesn't know how. Many parents will pick up the baby, rock, sing, pat, bounce, and offer a pacifier. That's a lot of soothing and a lot of associations that are dependent on you being there to provide them!

You should do the minimum necessary to soothe your baby back to sleep. At four weeks, you may need to soothe her until she settles, but maybe you can get by without the rocking, bouncing, and pacifier.

If you focus on this each night, by week six you'll be able to soothe your baby just by standing next to her and putting a hand lightly on her chest. You're effectively weaning her off this external source of stimulation by introducing as little of it in the first place as possible.

A Researcher's Perspective: The Discovery of Self-Soothers

In the late 1960s, a young psychiatrist named Thomas Anders was studying infant sleep patterns in the newborn nursery of Montefiore Hospital in New York City.

He used what was then a brand-new technology: time-lapse video. Watching these videos of babies sleeping, Anders could easily differentiate active sleep from quiet sleep. As he watched these tapes, Anders noticed something totally new and unexpected. He noticed that every single baby woke up at least a few times during the night, even the ones who had appeared to be "sleeping through the night." Before this discovery, sleep researchers assumed that babies who slept through the night really did just that—sleep the entire time. Instead, Anders found that all babies woke up at some point during the night.

All the babies in Anders's studies woke during the night, but what differed was how they responded to an awakening. Some babies cried when they woke, and Anders labeled these babies "signalers." Others woke, looked around, perhaps grabbing a teddy bear or sucking their thumbs, and then went back to sleep. Anders called these babies—the ones who didn't alert their parents to their awakenings—"self-soothers."

One study from Anders's lab showed that at 12 months of age, babies were more likely to be self-soothers if their parents waited just a few minutes before responding to their night wakings when they were three months of age. These parents weren't neglecting their babies; average wait time during this study was just 3 minutes.

Most babies have some ability to self-soothe, and this can develop further over time with some brief opportunities to practice.

—Alice Callahan, PhD, *The Science of Mom*

Five Minutes of Crying

When your baby starts crying, set a timer for five minutes.

That's how long to wait before you open the door of the nursery. Sometimes, your baby will still be crying after five minutes, and then you'll go in and soothe her. But eventually, your baby will stop crying during those five minutes. At least once. And that's enough to start the process of learning to self-soothe.

These are important moments when she experiences a small amount of discomfort, soothes herself, and then decides whether to go back to sleep or continue fussing. Eventually, your baby will be able to cry for a couple of minutes and then go right back to sleep.

This will happen in the absence of anything specifically wrong. She will simply wake up when one of her 45-minute cycles is over, let out a few cries, and then put herself back to sleep. That linking of separate sleep cycles is one of the most important skills your baby needs to teach herself.

This five-minute waiting period gives her the opportunity to learn that skill without escalating into frantic wailing. It's also a manageable period of time for parents, who will likely feel very uneasy about even five minutes of crying.

An Author's Perspective: Bringing up Bébé's La Pause

This pause—I'm tempted to call it *La Pause*—is crucial... using it very early on makes a big difference in how babies sleep. The parents who were a little less responsive to late-night fussing always had kids who were good sleepers, while the jumpy folks had kids who would wake up repeatedly at night until it became unbearable.

One reason for pausing is that young babies make a lot of movements and noise while they're sleeping. This is normal and fine.

Another reason for pausing is that babies wake up between their sleep cycles, which lasts about 2 hours. It's normal for them to cry a bit when they're first learning to connect these cycles. If a parent automatically interprets this cry as a demand for food or sign of distress and rushes in to soothe the baby, the baby will have a hard time learning to connect the cycles on his own. That is, he'll need an adult to come in and soothe him back to sleep at the end of each cycle.

Newborns typically can't connect sleep cycles on their own. But from about two or three months they usually can, if given a chance to learn how. Connecting sleep cycles is like riding a bike; if a baby manages to fall back to sleep on his own even once, he'll have an easier time doing it again the next time.

I'm not saying let your baby wail. Just give your baby a chance to learn.

This singular instruction could solve the mystery of why French parents claim they never let their babies cry for long periods. If parents do "The Pause" in baby's first two months, the baby can learn to fall back to sleep on his own. So his parents won't need to resort to "crying-it-out" later on.

—Pamela Druckerman, *Bringing Up Bébé*

A Pediatrician's Perspective: You Don't Have To Respond Just Because the Baby Woke Up

When you have a new baby in the house, your antennae for sound goes way up. You can hear your baby open her eyes. But that's not when you go feed her. Just because she's awake doesn't mean she needs you yet. You stay in your bed. You don't interact with the baby.

So the baby starts to cry a little bit. Stay patient. Just as the baby's starting to wail, then you go soothe.

Now, I understand there are some babies for whom when they start really, really wailing, it's hard to get them then to settle down. But you can learn the difference between wailing and fussing. When they're fussing, they're learning to self-soothe. Give them a chance. And continue to give them that chance night after night. That's parenting. A hundred opportunities before your baby eventually learns.

—Eileen Aicardi, M.D.

A Pediatrician's Perspective: Not All Noises that Sleeping Babies Make Are Cries for Help

Other parents find that if they let their baby squirm and fuss a bit, baby is able to resettle without intervention. This is a waking-by-waking call. It helps to remember that not all noises that sleeping babies make are cries for help. If you think your baby can settle himself back to sleep, delay rushing in and picking him up. Give him a chance to work things out on his own. He will let you know if he needs help.

—William Sears, M.D., *The Baby Sleep Book*

Swaddling

We love, love, love swaddling. In recent years, parents have realized that their babies sleep much longer when they are swaddled on a nightly basis. It's now fairly common practice to swaddle your baby at night for the first couple of months. If for some reason you hadn't assumed that you were going to swaddle your baby at night, we'll offer some brief rationale and then make a few recommendations.

At night, you're trying to limit the total amount of stimulation that your baby experiences. Both a pitch-dark room and loud white noise create an environment with low levels of stimulation. Similarly, swaddling significantly reduces the physical stimulation that can prevent your baby from transitioning from one sleep cycle to the next. A non-swaddled baby wakes up, starts flailing his arms, and can easily hit himself in the face or scratch his own skin, which creates a new irritation that will prevent him from settling down. A swaddled baby, protected from self-inflicted agitation has a much higher chance of simply staying asleep.

A Researcher's Perspective: Swaddled Infants Sleep Significantly Longer

The study showed that when infants between six and 16 weeks of age sleep swaddled and supine, they sleep longer, spend more time in NREM sleep, and awake less spontaneously than when not swaddled.

—*Pediatrics Journal,* May 2005

We found that there are three reasons parents who are intent on swaddling stop doing it. We want to address each of these in case they happen to you.

The first is that your baby may struggle against the swaddle while you're putting it on, causing you to think he's uncomfortable or resistant. This is completely normal. Babies struggle against everything; you'll find the same happens when you take their onesie off and on as well. So before giving up too early, commit to swaddling for at least one full week and pay less attention to how your baby responds to getting *into* the swaddle and more attention to how he seems once he's settled. You'll likely see an increase in your baby's contentment in having less movement available. And ultimately this is the goal: your baby associates this tight, closed-in feeling (similar to the small confines of the womb) with sleep.

The second reason is that you may find the hospital-style, triangle-folding maneuver is too hard to get right. You may have read about it in some pamphlet or practiced it in a pre-birthing class, but every brand-new parent finds that the triangle-swaddling maneuver is inconsistent at best. It just looks so easy when you see a nurse who has done it 10,000 times before do it for your baby: the end result is a perfectly snug, not-to-be-loosened triangle-swaddle fold.

So, skip that standard hospital blanket-swaddle altogether and jump straight to one of the products that are specifically designed to make this easier.

There are many versions. But whether they use Velcro or arm flaps, they're dramatically easier to get right, and they hold much better over the course of the night. Perhaps the most important reason to use them is that they're often designed with a large leg cavity that is accessible for diaper changes without removing the swaddle.

Finally, the third reason sometimes people don't use the swaddle is they think their baby doesn't like it because she successfully breaks out of it. A swaddle that doesn't stay tight throughout the entire night is one that was never put on correctly. Your baby's arms should be straight by their sides (or crossed over their chest, depending on the style of swaddle) and she should wake in the morning in the same position you left her in. So if your baby is successfully breaking out of the swaddle, that's a key sign that you should purchase one of the products that helps you do this consistently.

An Author's Perspective: Swaddling Doesn't Hurt a Baby's Hips

Antiquated wrapping techniques (with the knees and hips kept rigidly straight, or legs tightly bound with cloths or ropes) can hurt a baby's hips (developmental dysplasia of the hip, or DHH). But this has not been shown to be a risk with our modern style of swaddling as long as the hips have enough room to fully move.

The International Hip Dysplasia Institute says that swaddling is safe as long as the knees can flex and the hips can flex and open up easily.

—Harvey Karp, M.D., *The Happiest Baby Guide to Great Sleep*

3. Low-stimulation Soothing

The goal is for your baby to be able to put himself back to sleep with the least amount of soothing necessary. You won't be removing your intervention 100 percent; you'll still be there at first, just doing gradually less. This is much different from the philosophy of suddenly training your baby not to depend on you at all.

Think of it like teaching a kid how to ride a bike. You start with a tricycle that is impossible to tip over, and then you move onto training wheels, and finally to chasing your child around the schoolyard while he toddles on two wheels. Your goal in training your kid how to ride a bike is to get her past each step and enabling her to need your help as little as possible. Plenty of parents have learned the art of barely touching that bike, as they're simultaneously trying to help their child establish a sense of balance, while also trying to prevent a tooth-chipping crash. It's a parental art form.

The method of crying-it-out is like taking the training wheels off and saying, "Good luck!" The Dream Feed Method is much more like, "I'm here to help you if you start to fall, but I'm not going to pedal the bike for you."

What follows are several types of intervention. When your baby is crying, your goal is to intervene as little as possible while still coaxing him back to sleep. Off-schedule feeding stops the crying right away but totally disrupts all sleep-training progress. High-stimulation comfort includes rocking, swaying, bouncing, and so on. They work, but cannot be duplicated by your baby independently. If you are disciplined in only using them when necessary, your baby won't learn to depend on them.

Low-stimulation comfort includes placing a hand on your baby or even just sitting there quietly. It's the lightest possible touch. These are the little acts of comfort that still give your baby plenty of opportunity to practice her own self-soothing.

A Pediatrician's Perspective: No Middle-of-the-Night Entertainment Please

No middle-of-the-night entertainment, please. You're there as a comforter, not a playmate. Nighttime is for sleeping, not for playing. If baby needs your help to resettle, try to do it quickly, calmly, and comfortably. Even though you're what we dub the "Caribbean approach"—"no problem, baby." If baby senses your anxiety and irritation, she is less likely to resettle. Try to resettle baby with a simple song or patting with your hands. If you need to pick up baby for a bit of swaying or rocking, don't make the routine too interesting. Your goal is to lull her back to sleep.

—William Sears, M.D., *The Baby Sleep Book*

Off-Schedule Feeding

Breastfeeding solves just about everything. The baby is cuddled up next to your skin, sucking on a nipple, and swallowing warm milk. A crying baby in almost every circumstance can be settled by offering her the breast. There will be many parents who simply decide to always use this type of soothing.

There's no need for us to debate the merits of that decision. All parents get to make their own decision. Our recommendation for those that choose to follow the Dream Feed Method is to use breastfeeding as a scheduled form of nourishment. Help your baby learn that the next meal is going to come no matter what, without needing to cry for it.

Breastfeeding, off-schedule, in response to crying, creates the expectation that crying should always produce the next meal. It also creates the expectation that crying when her stomach is only 50 percent empty will immediately produce more milk. Which then turns feedings into non-stop snacking. Our goal in teaching your baby to self-soothe is to consider nursing as a time to eat full meals, not a form of snacking in order to soothe herself.

A Researcher's Perspective: Adopt a Parent-lite Approach

Minimize sleep transitions that involve parental assistance and allow a child to achieve and maintain sleep alone. Adopt a "parent-lite" approach to sleep achievement. Be there and be supportive, but keep it minimal rather than the reverse. The baby needs to feel your love and support, but when it's time to be asleep, leave them alone to finalize the last steps of sleep achievement. As a parent, you have a major and positive role to play when the baby is ready to be finally asleep, these events are best managed by the baby alone. This is true from birth.

—Brian Symon, M.D.

Rocking, Singing, Swaying in Your Arms

Believe it or not, rocking, swaying, and singing seem to be at the epicenter of the fight between the attachment parents and the cry-it-outers.

The attachment parents believe you should love your baby and keep him close: rock, sway, and sing as an expression of unqualified motherly love. To which the cry-it-outers respond with their black-and-white assessment that if you don't break your child of their attachment, you are signing up for a lifetime of middle-of-the-night shenanigans.

Let's see if we can satisfy both worlds with a reasonable alternative.

For the most part, the Dream Feed Method allows you to listen to your motherly instincts and soothe, guilt-free and without fear of creating these so-called dangerous, negative, sleeping-soothing associations. First, with the Dream Feed Method, you're ideally spending less time trying to get your baby back to sleep in those middle of the night hours because you are pre-empting her agitation with dream feeds that keep her from fully waking in the first place. This whole conflict about rocking, swaying, and singing just shouldn't matter as much.

As we've already discussed, in the morning, when you're trying to hold your baby off until the 7:00 a.m., you'll employ every soothing trick out there except for a feeding. Rock, sway, and sing away. You're not trying to get your baby back to sleep; you're just trying to get him to adjust to lasting a few more minutes before the next feeding.

With that said, there are still some best practices. If your baby never learns how to fall asleep any other way than being rocked, swayed, and sung to, then, yes, that will become an association that can be difficult to break.

So, try this. Start soothing with as much rocking, singing, and swaying as you like and then transition toward less and less movement. After a few minutes, slow down the swaying and the rocking. A few minutes later put her down while still awake and place a hand softly on her chest while she lies in the crib. Continue with this transition until you start dropping certain steps (e.g., maybe you pat her bottom lightly before setting her in the crib, but you never sway).

You'll find that a light amount of soothing, or as we refer to it, low-stimulation soothing, is actually a wonderful way to interact with your baby at night. It doesn't feel like an extra 30-minute quads workout bouncing your baby, nor does it feel like you're not allowed to touch her when she's upset. It's just a gentle transition from calming your baby down for her, to watching as she learns to mostly calm herself.

A Researcher's Perspective: Of Course There Will Be Times...

To the best of your ability, allow your baby to achieve sleep and maintain sleep independently as often as possible. Of course the baby will go to sleep in your arms on occasion or over dad's shoulder or being rocked, and that's fine, BUT decrease these events, rather than allowing them to build up until they become the norm. You will know that there is a problem when the baby settles as soon as he is picked up and cries as soon as he is put down again.

—Brian Symon, M.D.

Vibrating Rockers

There is a reason every mother loves these.

They combine both rocking and vibration, and when motorized, they become a 'set-it-and-forget-it' form of soothing. Babies that often fall asleep in these devices learn to associate the vibration with relaxing into a sleep state. Before you realize what has happened, your baby will struggle to fall asleep *without* that vibration.

If you do choose to use a vibrating chair or rocker (and we know many mothers who have successfully navigated this temptation), we propose a middle ground: Use them only in the daytime, and stick with the old fashioned bassinet at night. Vibrating chairs can be a great tool to use when you want to get something done or enjoy a meal. Using them for naps here and there is fine, too. But by maintaining consistent nighttime associations (dark room, still bassinet, white noise), your baby will differentiate the vibrating chair from something he needs to be able to sleep.

Caressing Your Baby in the Crib

Anytime you can avoid moving your swaddled baby out of the crib, you've taken a big step toward helping him self-soothe. But this can take a little bit of time. Get yourself a chair or stool, place it right next to the crib, and settle in.

Drape your arm over the crib railing and place your hand on your baby where he lays. Let him feel your hand on top of the swaddle, apply pressure, and lightly rock him from side to side if necessary—though if you can soothe your baby with a still hand, that's better than creating motion.

With your hand still, you can also decrease the pressure your baby feels over time so that, by the end, your hand is actually hovering over your baby, and all she's really using you for is your presence.

Holding Without Rocking Next to the Bed

If you've found your baby will not calm while laying in his crib with your hand on his chest, the next natural step is to pick him up. Even this can be done with varying levels of stimulation. You'll want to start with the lowest level. Lift your swaddled baby up, keeping him in the same position he was in the bed. Resist the temptation to sway or rock. All you're doing is using your proximity to calm him, while allowing him to figure out how to fall asleep by himself.

If your baby can't get all the way there himself, add in a little bit of swaying and rocking, and just smoothly decrease it until you're back to standing still.

> **A Pediatrician's Perspective: Try Your Favorite Sleep Cues**
>
> When baby stirs, gently lay your hands on her without picking her up. Stay with her and continue laying on a comforting hand as you say or sing your favorite sleep cues, such as "night-night" or "sleepy-sleepy." Stay with it until she settles. If she starts to wake up again right away, you can give it another try. Again lay your hands on her and give her your "sleepy-sleepy" sleep cue. If she just can't fall asleep, pick her up and walk around the bedroom for a while, holding her in a sleep-inducing position such as the neck nestle. By this time you will know whether you can

get her to stretch out her sleep more or whether it's simply time to feed her.

—Dr. William Sears, *The Baby Sleep Book*

An Author's Perspective: Just Being Close By Can Be Enough

When the baby is in the crib, reassure him that, although you are not going to pick him up, you are right there. Stand next to the crib, or sit on a glider ottoman or chair so you are close to the baby.

—Suzy Giordano, "The Baby Coach," *Twelve Hours' Sleep by Twelve Weeks Old*

4. Crib vs. Room-sharing vs. Co-sleeping

This one is entirely up to you.

The question of room sharing vs. co-sleeping has been debated ad nauseam. The reality is that the Dream Feed Method works, whether you choose to co-sleep, room-share, or use a separate room. This is a very personal decision and will be different for every family. We encourage you to choose what feels best. This being said, in our experience, the choice of sleeping arrangements does impact how easy the Dream Feed Method feels. The separate-room approach is by far the easiest, while room-sharing is sometimes a little more difficult. Co-sleeping presents a few more hurdles for Dream Feed Method parents, but it's still totally doable.

Whichever arrangement you decide to try, here are a few suggestions to keep your baby safe, most importantly, and to keep you on track with sleep training.

Options 1: Baby in a crib or bassinet in another room

Until 2016, having the baby in a crib or bassinet in another room had been the default recommendation by the American Academy of Pediatrics (AAP) for over a decade. It was believed during that time that babies sleeping in their own room had the lowest rates of SIDS and had the best opportunity to learn independent sleep. In 2016, this all changed when the AAP suddenly recommended bedside room-sharing. What they found was that a percentage of parents, small but not insignificant, were soothing their babies while sitting on a couch or in a rocking chair in the middle of the night. After months of sleepless nights, and hours upon hours of soothing that baby, sitting down on a comfortable couch proved irresistible and, tragically, some percentage of parents fell asleep on the couch with their babies suffocating below them.

This led the American Academy of Pediatrics to no longer recommending separate rooms. Most of the moms who succeeded with the Dream Feed Method before 2016, used separate rooms from the start, as was the formal recommendation then. These separate sleeping spaces made it far easier to resist soothing their baby at every little flutter of sound, and thus it was easier for their babies to learn self-soothing. Yes, it was harder to get out of bed and walk to a separate room several times a night. But what worked particularly well with this arrangement was that at least one parent got to sleep through the crying.

Probably the most common pattern we saw then and continue to see today is to start with some period of bedside room-sharing. It's just so easy in the beginning to have the baby close by, and there's just no concern of establishing a pattern in that first month. And so that is our recommendation for you: aim to move your baby to his independent room somewhere in the second month. This is also when you'll be starting to make real progress with the Dream Feed Method. Soon enough, your baby will be sleeping 6 to 8 hours in one stretch, and predictable dream feed times will be scheduled into the night. It's especially at this time that having your baby in a separate room makes sense.

Option 2: Room-sharing

For those doing bedside room-sharing, you are following the current recommendation of the American Academy of Pediatrics. You will find that it's easy to be there for your baby as she starts to wake up and need a feeding. The biggest thing to keep an eye on is your progress towards 3-hour scheduled feedings. If you're past the one-month stage for babies born at normal weight, and you're really struggling to get to 3-hour scheduled feedings, having the baby so close by may be part of the issue. It does take some time for babies to learn how to sleep for their typical 45 minutes, wake up like all babies do, fuss and fall back asleep without turning that fuss into a screaming wail.

The fact that some parents intervene during this process of learning how to link 45 minute sleep cycles is the entire basis for the dozens of books written about self-soothing. Some research has even said that simply waiting one or two minutes is enough for babies to learn how to fall back asleep between sleep cycles. But as any parent can tell you, two minutes of your baby crying just 18 inches away from you is pure torture.

So, be aware of this tension, as you pick the time that's right for you to move from bedside room-sharing to your baby's own crib in her own room. If you make it to 3-hour scheduled feedings and are starting to use the Dream Feed Method to lengthen the final sleep period with some level of consistency during the second month, then everything's working fine. Take a deep breath, keep doing what you're doing: it's working.

If you're struggling to get to that 3-hour scheduled sleep cycle, or you're unable to move past it with any regularity throughout the second month, and you've also observed that you can't restrain yourself from soothing your baby instantly, then it might be time to make a change.

Option 3: Co-sleeping

We have seen that it's harder for babies to complete the Dream Feed Method when they spend longer than a month or two co-sleeping. But we've also seen that it's possible. And if it's important to you to co-sleep, then you should do it. First, a few notes on safety. There is conflicting research on the relative safety of co-sleeping. Since others have explained it all so many times in so many ways, we won't dive deeply into it. But we'll summarize it with this. Initially, co-sleeping was correlated with higher rates of SIDS, which people blamed on suffocation from being stuck underneath the parents or the sheets.

However, when you factor out parents who drank or smoke cigarettes while co-sleeping, the differences went away completely. Co-sleeping has both been wildly popular in the U.S. and frowned upon by the American Academy of Pediatrics for decades. Internationally, co-sleeping is the default across much of the world. Taken together, if you know you're going to be drinking or smoking cigarettes, don't co-sleep. If you aren't going to be drinking or smoking cigarettes, and it's important to you to co-sleep, then do so as carefully as you can. And like the bedside room-shares, just keep an eye on your sleep-training progress. If you find that you're unable to get to 3-hour scheduled feedings, consider moving away from co-sleeping. If you do successfully get to the 3-hour scheduled feedings and are making meaningfully consistent progress in the second month, then the co-sleeping is working out just fine for you.

A Researcher's Perspective: How to Make Bed Sharing Safer

If, despite the concerns, you decide to bed-share, you'll want to do everything possible to reduce the hazards. These tips can help stack the deck in your baby's favor and significantly lower the risks.

SAFE BED

- Don't sleep on a waterbed, air mattress, or living room furniture.

- Be sure there are no spaces between the mattress and the wall, bed frame, or headboard that could trap your baby's head.

SAFE BEDDING

- Use only a sheet on your bed—no pillow, duvet, bumpers, stuffed animals, or positioners.

- If your room is cold, dress your baby comfortably, but avoid overheating. (Touch his ears and nose; they should feel neither cold nor hot.)

SAFE BEDMATES

- Don't let your baby share a bed with a smoker, pet, sibling, or someone who is obese or profoundly tired.

- Keep your baby next to one parent, not between both of you.

- Never use alcohol or drugs (including antihistamines) that can reduce your ability to sense your baby and react to his needs.

SAFE BABY

- Always place your baby on his back.

- Breast-feed if you can.

- Offer a bedtime pacifier.

- Don't bed-share with a preemie or a low-birth-weight baby.

SAFE ROOM

- Keep the temperature between 66°F and 72°F (19°C–22°C).

- Ventilate your room well.

- Don't use candles, incense, or a wood fire.

SAFE SWADDLING

- Snugly wrap your baby in a large, light blanket to help him from accidentally rolling over or unraveling his blanket during sleep.

—Dr. Harvey Karp, *The Happiest Baby Guide to Great Sleep*

Anything Goes in the First Month

Yes, establishing your newborn in her own crib, in her own room makes for easier sleep training.

However, you can still get there if you co-sleep or room-share. If you want the best of both worlds, try co-sleeping or room-sharing and then make the move after four weeks. There will be no impact on your sleep training success if you wait four to six weeks before establishing your baby in a separate room.

A Pediatrician's Perspective: There's No One Answer to Co-sleeping

I think ultimately you do what feels comfortable to you as a parent, and as a couple. The whole issue of co-sleeping is very cultural. Certainly, there are cultures where everybody sleeps in the same bed. And if culturally that's where you're from, then you do what you feel comfortable doing.

The first couple of weeks, you do whatever you need to do to survive, and if that means that the baby sleeps between you and your partner, you do it.

My preference is that the baby be in a co-sleeper or a bassinet that is placed right next to the mom so that she has easy access. I always caution against sleeping with the baby on your chest. After a couple of weeks, as the baby begins to get older, be careful giving her access to the buffet table all night long. That does not help the baby to learn to sleep without food for longer stretches.

When babies can hear you, smell you, see you in the middle of the night, they often times will cry and cry and cry and not take no for an answer. It's hard not to respond to that. So I recommend moving the baby out of the room sometime in the first 3 to 4 months.

The Academy of Pediatrics has now recommended that babies sleep in the parents' room for one year. The recommendation for many years used to be that, if possible, it was good to get the baby out of the parental room, but now that has flipped. It just doesn't make sense to me. I think it makes it really hard for anyone to get good sleep at night, and I think, ultimately, at some point, mothers and fathers need to be able to say that their sleep is important too.

—Eileen Aicardi, M.D.

5. A Dark, Loud Nursery

Preparing the nursery is one of the more fun parts of anticipating your baby's arrival. In addition to purchasing the crib, picking out colors, and opening all of those baby shower gifts, take some time to focus on two key aspects of the nursery that will aid with sleep training:

1. Making the room dark
2. Incorporating loud white noise

Total Darkness

Most parents don't actually believe in total darkness because they have childhood memories of night-lights.

You can bring in night-lights when your child is a little bit older. But when they are newborns straight from the hospital and trying to learn how to self-soothe, you want to approximate as closely as possible what they are used to experiencing—which is 100 percent absolute, total darkness.

To achieve this, you'll likely need total blackout shades. It's time to get obsessive here. Make sure that you don't have light creeping in through the bottom, sides, or top. And don't overlook those tiny lights on any electronics that will be in the nursery. While those lights seem small during the daytime, they light up an otherwise dark room. Cover them with black electrical tape.

Dim, Red Light

It doesn't just matter how dim your light source is, it's also about the color of the bulb. The blue part of the light spectrum is the part that is most jarring to the eyes at night. You've probably recognized that when you look at your phone in a dark room, it's actually painful on your eyes. Even worse for our purposes, the blue in the light spectrum is what signals the body that it's time to wake up. When your baby experiences the tiniest amount of the blue light spectrum, his body interprets it as the beginning of sunrise. This is, of course, *not* the message you want to send at 2:00 a.m.

To solve this, you must block the blue wave spectrum from your light source, which will then make your light appear red. While you still want to keep the light as dim as possible, using a zero blue light source is much better than using any normal yellow or white light source, even if that normal light source is significantly dimmer. By using a red bulb, you can actually turn the light up a little brighter without negatively impacting your baby's sleep pattern. This enables middle-of-the-night diaper changes without stimulating your baby more than necessary.

There are two products you are going to want to buy. Both are made by a company called Low Blue Lights (http://lowbluelights.com), which we've worked with and known about for years. This first product was built as a book light. It's actually the perfect changing table light. It is an unbelievably small light bulb put through a blue-light-blocking lens. You can safely work on changing your baby without having to hold anything and without the light getting in his eyes.

The second product you'll want is a super tiny red LED flashlight that sits on top of a 9-volt battery. It blocks the blue light and serves as your flashlight when you are in the nursery.

Loud White Noise

You should have a white noise machine. Remember the goal is not silence— the goal is to mimic the atmosphere of the womb, which is a fairly loud and consistent whooshing sound. The added benefit of a loud white noise machine is that it will drown out any sounds from outside of the nursery.

A Researcher's Perspective: White Noise Works Miracles

White noise works miracles with fussy babies and is an amazingly powerful cue to boost baby sleep. This special sound is as important as swaddling.

The sound needed to turn on the *calming reflex* when the baby's crying is a rough, rumbly whoosh noise that's as loud as his crying.

Once your baby is calm, lower the level of your white noise to about the loudness of a shower (65–70 decibels) to keep the calming reflex on.

And to help your baby doze off easily and sleep soundly, white noise is a must. The best white noise for sleeping mimics the sound babies hear in the womb.

—Dr. Harvey Karp, M.D., *The Happiest Baby Guide to Great Sleep*

Nursery Checklist

There is no end to checklists of everything you'll want for your nursery, so we're not going to repeat that entire list here. But we have included a list of specific items you'll want to consider buying to aid sleep training. We mention these throughout the book.

We've organized these by goal, and each gives a description of what it will help you accomplish.

Goal: Make the Nursery Pitch Black

Blackout curtains

- Don't trust your normal curtains to block out enough light. If you can see any light at all through the curtains, then they're not blackout curtains. Additionally, you want to make sure that light is not seeping in from above, below, and along the sides of the curtains.

- You can buy blackout curtain liners that will go inside your existing curtain. You can also replace your existing curtain rod with a dual curtain rod: one that holds the blackout curtain liner and the other that holds your existing curtains. One nice trick is to tape the curtain liner to the outside edges of your window to prevent the light from coming in through the sides, while still making it possible to open and close the middle.

- Alternatively you can buy travel blackout curtains which can be affixed either with suction cups or Velcro and they can block out the light completely as well, although they're not as easy to take off and on if you plan to let light in during the day. For many parents, the nursery simply becomes a place that you'll want to have constantly at the ready for sleeping. So completely blocking out your window at least for the first four months is not a bad idea.

Black electrical tape

- Every little device has a small but bright indicator light. They'll seem insignificant during the daytime, but at nighttime it's just enough stimulation to keep your newborn focused on it instead of drifting back to sleep. Simply tape over these lights with a small piece of black electrical tape.

Red reading light bulb and a dimmer switch

- You can simply put a red bulb into your existing lamp (look for the same bulbs that are used in photography dark rooms). Those light bulbs are filtering out the blue wavelength that specifically stimulates wakefulness. It is much more important to filter out the blue wavelength light than it is to simply dim the light with a lower wattage bulb. If you combine a red incandescent light bulb with an adjustable dimmer switch, you can effectively make it such that during nighttime feedings, you will have filtered out all the blue wavelength and dimmed down the remaining light close to nothing. You're eyes will need to adjust before you can find your way around the room, but this is one of the greatest little tricks for making that 7:00 p.m. bedtime process go smoothly.

Red book light

- Similarly, you'll want something for the diaper-changing area that can be focused directly on the diaper area, without shining in your baby's eyes. And again you'll want to omit any blue wavelength light by using a red light bulb. A book light can be perfect for this because it can attach right to your changing station and the flexible neck can bend away from your baby's eyes.

Nine-volt battery red LED flashlight

- To complete our trifecta of low-wattage red lights, this is just a tiny little red LED bulb that sits on top of a 9-volt battery. It is just enough light to have in your hands when you walk into the bedroom late at night and don't want to disturb your baby as you're preparing to offer a dream feed. They're affordable, and you can have a few of them lying around so that anyone walking around late at night doesn't have to turn on lights.

Goal: Fill Your Nursery with Only White Noise

White noise machine

- Pick a white noise machine that generates a fairly loud white noise. The key to a white noise machine is that it is capable of generating a low pitch sound. You are trying to mimic the sound the baby heard while in the womb. Be picky in your search. Many come with all sorts of night-lights built in. Make sure you can either turn the light off or you will need to tape over it with black tape.

Baby 'shusher'

- Also buy a baby shusher, which is louder than your all-night white noise machine but generally only works for a small period of time (15 to 30 minutes). It can be helpful for settling your baby down. Once settled, you'll likely prefer a slightly quieter white noise machine for the rest of the night.

Under-door foam draft guards

- These are actually not to block the draft, but to block the light and sounds flowing in from underneath the door. Usually this is just a tube of foam that slides right underneath your door.

- Additionally, look into soundproofing material for any areas that are letting in sound. Give yourself permission to be obsessive. You want this nursery to be a cocoon.

Goal: Swaddles Galore

Swaddle blanket

- We mentioned this earlier: way too many parents struggle with the traditional swaddle blanket, unable to get the triangle fold perfect. Leave the perfect swaddling technique to the nurses at the hospital. Get yourself something easier that works every time.

- Look for the swaddles with arm flaps that make it easy to successfully swaddle your child every time. These also have a large pouch for the legs, so that they are free to move about (which is good). Some people also like the Velcro swaddling products, though oftentimes they require you to cinch them incredibly tight for them to work at all. Double check that the swaddling product you use allows you to change the diaper without undoing the swaddle completely.

- Also be prepared to upgrade your style of swaddle as your baby grows. Many parents find that Velcro swaddles work well in the early weeks, but graduate to something stronger (often the arm-flap style) as their baby gets a little older.

Goal: Cribs and Bassinets

Bassinet

- If your stroller came with a bassinet certified for sleeping, it will actually work for the full nighttime for at least the first month or two. Babies like how small they are. Double check that it's certified for sleeping. That simply means it has passed tests to make sure that the mattress and bassinet sides are breathable.

Crib

- The same goes for your crib. Pay extra special attention to the ratings of the mattress. Some are much better in SIDS reduction than others. Remember nothing else goes in the crib other than the baby. No stuffed animals, blankets, or bumpers.

Wedge

- Consider a wedge to be placed underneath the bassinet or crib mattress. For babies with reflux or excessive gassiness, a 15-degree tilt is enough to help them sleep right through it.

Stool

- Find a trusty stool to place next to the crib. You simply want something that allows you to sit there with your arm resting gently on your baby for an extended period of time.

Goal: Check In Without Opening the Door

HD camera

- Buy the great HD camera. You want to be able to satisfy your peace of mind and monitor your baby closely without having to open the door. The products and technology are changing every year. Just buy something that gives you true HD vision, incorporates night vision, and is Internet-connected, so you can see your baby from anywhere.

Breathing monitor

- Here again, the technology is changing pretty fast. One type of breathing monitor places two extremely sensitive pads underneath your baby's mattress, which measure the vibration of her breathing. If it can't sense that vibration in 20 seconds, it lets out a loud alarm. You have to remember to turn it off every time you pick up your baby in the middle of the night, which is actually an easy enough pattern to establish for yourself. Even so, you'll probably have at least one false alarm to chill your blood. But in the event that some piece of clothing or swaddle someday comes loose and obstructs your baby's airflow, that alarm will notify you in time. More likely, this device will satisfy your anxiety. Absent an alarm going off, you know your baby is breathing and you don't have to open the door to check.

- There are also some new products that are attempting to measure oxygen levels in your baby's blood more directly, which is the technology the hospitals use when premature babies are in the nursery. Some of them fit right into a custom baby sock. Again the technology is changing quickly, so do your homework.

- Some baby video cameras are attempting to incorporate breathing monitoring features, which would allow a computer inside the video camera to detect that breathing has ceased and alert you. This is a promising concept but at the time of publishing, we haven't yet seen a proven product.

- Lastly, keep an eye on reviews of the latest research in mattress vibration. There are a few interesting products in development that are attempting to aid in sleep training by gently vibrating the mattress to soothe a restless baby, a practice that has already proven to solve sleep terrors in babies and children.

For every one of these items, you can find up-to-date reviews on our website.

6. Problems and Solutions

Difficulty Falling Asleep at 7:00 p.m.

There are some babies who, right from the start, have great difficulty going down. And there are others who may have gone down easily for a month or two, and then all of a sudden struggle for the first hour of the night.

There are two dangers you face when this pattern emerges.

The first is that bedtime turns into a multi-hour process. There is no temperament of baby that exists that requires this, but you can slip into this pattern if you're not careful.

The second danger you face is that you become tempted to soothe your baby to sleep in your arms, only placing her in her crib once she is fast asleep. While this feels great in the short term, it creates an association you won't be able to keep up forever. Putting your baby down in her crib awake and letting her put herself to sleep *is* achievable even if it doesn't feel like that right now. If your baby doesn't learn this skill now, the result will be that going to bed will always be met with long periods of crying.

If your baby is having difficulty going to sleep at 7:00 p.m., go through the checklist and make sure you are doing all of the fundamentals:

- The room is pitch black.

- The white noise is loud enough.

- You are feeding the baby until she is full, including a top-up bottle.

- You change and swaddle your baby before the feeding starts.

- You burp your baby when you're 75 percent done feeding.

- You transfer her immediately from the feeding to the crib.

- The swaddle is tight with the arms straight.

If you are doing all of this—and have been doing all of this consistently—and you are still struggling, then of course you're going to have to find additional ways to help soothe your baby. This is where you'll leverage those low-stimulation soothing techniques.

In the best-case scenario, you can calm your baby simply by sitting next to her or by resting a hand on her chest.

The next best scenario is that, in addition to the above, you also hold a pacifier in her mouth. Remember, in a couple of months, the pacifier will be replaced by her sucking on her hand to soothe herself, so it's actually a fairly positive form of soothing for this stage.

If you do need to pick your baby up, you'll do so while staying right next to the crib, and while it will try your patience, your goal is to calm your baby down and then put her back into in the crib before she falls asleep in your arms.

An Author's Perspective: Put Your Baby Down While She Is Still Awake

You have to put the baby in the crib while she is still awake. This is because the baby has to learn to put herself to sleep in order to be able to sleep through the night. After the baby has learned to fall asleep in the crib on her own for at least 6 weeks, it is fine to have her fall asleep in your arms one or two times per week, but not two nights in a row. Otherwise, the baby could develop the habit of falling asleep outside the crib and then not be able to fall asleep on her own in the crib.

—Suzy Giordano, "The Baby Coach," *Twelve Hours' Sleep by Twelve Weeks Old*

Fifteen Minutes of Crying To Fall Asleep

Even if you do everything right, there are still going to be times when you have to listen to your baby cry as he puts himself to sleep. Again, this is different from crying-it-out, where your baby cries for hours and eventually gives up from exhaustion.

Sometimes there won't be any crying at all. Your baby will simply go to sleep instantly. Oftentimes, you'll have a couple of minutes of crying as she gets herself comfortable. But you need to be prepared for as much as 15 minutes of crying.

Early on, before your baby has learned self-soothing, 15 minutes of crying would just lead to more crying. There wasn't going to be an end to it, because your baby had not learned to soothe himself.

But you've observed that your baby can cry, then calm back down, and ultimately go to sleep. This has likely happened in the middle of the night; now, you'll watch it play out at bedtime. Your goal is to be able to leave the room with your baby still awake, because that is the essential skill your baby needs to continue to develop.

There is nothing magical about the 15-minute dividing line—we offer it more as guidance. The important part is that you resist the temptation to 'solve' the falling asleep process for your baby. You'll find this phase is short-lived; before long he'll be confidently putting himself to sleep.

A Researcher's Perspective: Some Babies Go to Sleep More Quickly If Left to Cry for a While

Sometimes, if all else fails, the best approach is simply to leave the baby alone. Many babies cannot fall asleep without crying, and will go to sleep more quickly if left to cry for a while.

—American Academy of Pediatrics

Overtiredness

It's counterintuitive at first, but newborns struggle to sleep when they're *too* tired. When they become overtired, newborns get fussier and struggle to calm themselves down.

So don't keep your newborn up during the day thinking she'll sleep better at night.

> ### A Researcher's Perspective: Put Your Baby to Sleep Before She's Exhausted
>
> The Golden Moment: Put your baby to sleep before she's exhausted. Most people think a baby's ready for slumber when her eyes get lidded and her head slumps against our shoulder. Actually, at that point she is overtired.
>
> —Dr. Harvey Karp, M.D., *The Happiest Baby Guide to Great Sleep*

In fact, babies who sleep well during the day usually sleep well during the night. And likewise, babies who don't sleep well during the day struggle to sleep well at night.

Keeping to a daytime and nighttime schedule prevents over-tiredness. The regularity ensures that you're not trying to put your baby down to sleep past the point of exhaustion. But in the inevitable event that this does happen, the solution in the moment is to reduce stimulation. Stimulation in this case includes sounds, light, rocking, singing, bouncing, etc.

Also, work to create a smooth transition to sleep. Going directly into a dark room, full of white noise, swaddled, and putting her down immediately into her bassinet may be too much of a shift. Instead, you'll want to settle her down and move more gradually toward the low-stimulation environment.

So, start your feeding with the lights on and as your baby begins to feed, turn the lights off and the white noise on.

A Researcher's Perspective: There's Nothing Else that Can Help with Overtiredness

The baby will cry. Do nothing. Hold each other's hands, play cards, watch TV, but do not pick up the baby.

The baby will cry. The crying will be loud and long. It can last for a very long time. The more overtired a baby, the longer she can cry, until exhaustion takes over.

Most parents find this instruction difficult to obey. On the surface it appears unkind to leave the baby crying. You will need to have faith in me for the moment. This does work, and is not unloving. In fact the reverse is the case: helping the child to "learn" good sleep habits is one of the kindest, most loving things you will ever do for your baby.

After a short time many parents break and "give comfort." This can be disastrous. Even if the baby stops crying in a parent's arms, at some time she has to be put down. Let's say the parents spend 15 minutes settling the baby. Eventually, the baby goes back into the cot and starts to cry again. All that has been achieved is that the baby is now a further 15 minutes or more deprived of sleep.

—Brian Symon, M.D.

PART 5:

After Sleep Training

Parents can only give good advice or
put them on the right paths,
but the final forming of a person's
character lies in their own hands.

—Anne Frank

Congratulations!

First and foremost: you made it. Your baby is successfully sleeping 12 hours a night, from dusk till dawn.

We have a few maintenance suggestions for you, but, in large part, if your baby is sleeping dusk till dawn by the fourth month, you are done. That routine will settle and become quite stable. Give yourself the next few weeks to really make sure that it's locked in, but then you should explore and enjoy the flexibility that your hard work has provided.

You have a daytime nap routine now, but don't consider yourself locked into it. Feel free to skip naps if you're off having fun or let your kiddo grab a partial nap in the car on the way back. It shouldn't really disrupt his nighttime sleep schedule. Feel free to travel, and whenever you change time zones, just jump onto the new time zone. You should be able to jump back to your normal routine after you return. Take a much-deserved night off—leave the little one with a babysitter, grandparents, siblings... You'll of course give them instructions, so they're following your routines, but don't fret about it. There's nothing a grandparent can do in one night to screw up your sleep-training progress.

And if ever you go a little too far in your flexibility, you should be able to get right back to where you are now. It should even get easier to put your baby down at night. You may have a fairly involved routine right now, but because you've established the practice of putting your baby in the crib while she is still awake, you can continue that all the way through infancy, toddlerhood, and childhood.

When your child is healthy, you should still stay pretty firm about no feeding between 7:00 p.m. and 7:00 a.m. There's really no reason for it. As long as you don't mess with the expectation of food at night, your baby's sleep-training success should be fairly locked in for years.

Here are a few other sleep-related milestones to look forward to:

Currently your baby is at either two or three naps a day. At some point, you'll reduce that to two naps, and then down to one nap, and eventually none. From our sleep-training perspective, it doesn't really matter when that is, so feel free to go along with whatever fits best in your child-care plan. Usually your nanny or daycare will have some opinion about daytime naps. Your baby is going to be so well rested at night that she'll adapt to anything during the day.

You also don't need to think too hard about transitioning from crib to toddler bed and so on. Do whatever is most convenient in your life. It shouldn't have an effect on your sleep-training success. In general, more time in the crib is easier on the parents because you don't have to worry about your baby leaving the safety of the crib and exploring a potentially not perfectly child-proofed room or home.

Hold fast to the 7:00 a.m. start of the day, even when your baby is old enough to get out of bed by himself. Because you worked so hard to prevent that 5:00 a.m. wakeup time, your baby should be perfectly fine entertaining himself if he wakes up early. Stoplight alarm clocks are also a great way to teach your growing child when it's okay to get up and leave his room.

If a second baby is in your plans, our recommendation is to try to keep the children sleeping in separate rooms for the first four months so that you can focus on the Dream Feed Method. But after that, it's totally fine to bring them together for nighttime sleeping.

Don't Be Afraid to Start Solids

For babies sleeping 12 hours a night and growing like crazy, their appetite during the day is also going to grow. Remember, the total calories taken in per 24-hour period don't change when your baby sleeps longer at night. That means that more calories need to be backed into the daytime feeds. Introducing solids, when you and your doctor feel the time is right, is a great way to help fill your baby's belly as a supplement to your own breastfeeding goals.

A Researcher's Perspective: Introduce Solids When You Are Ready

Starting allergenic solids from 16 weeks has now been proven to decrease the frequency of food allergies. The UK LEAP study has made a huge contribution to infant well-being in this regard.

Babies learn, or more accurately, the gut "learns" about the foods in the environment. The earlier in life that this happens, the more likely the gut is to recognize a new food protein as an energy source rather than a toxic object to which an immune reaction would occur.

Current recommendations are to start allergenic foods, such as say peanut butter, from about 4 months.

—Brian Symon, M.D.

A Pediatrician's Perspective: Start Solids in Months Four to Six

Around four to six months, babies start to watch people eating. They stare, opening their mouths with curiosity. Parents can offer a taste of anything soft directly from their own plate. There is no necessary order of food introduction, time of the day, amount of food, or food exclusions. (Except raw honey, which should be avoided for now.) The current recommendation is to offer highly allergenic foods like peanut butter or almond butter early on to help decrease the likelihood of allergies later in childhood.

—Eileen Aicardi, M.D.

The Dreaded Sleep Regressions

For parents who elect another style of sleep training (cry-it-out), there is lots of talk about specific sleep regressions: at four months, six months, ten months, 12 months and 18 months. As we stated much earlier, with the Dream Feed Method there aren't any regressions. Your baby's sleep patterns around the fourth month are imprinted and actually become very stable. If you succeeded at the Dream Feed Method and your baby is sleeping from dusk till dawn by the end of the fourth month, take everything you read about sleep regressions with a grain of salt; it shouldn't apply to your baby.

Our key piece of guidance here is to not ascribe a change in your baby's sleep behavior as an unavoidable regression. If you stay relatively consistent, your baby should be sleeping from dusk till dawn right through his infant, toddler, and pre-school years. And while that sleep schedule is fairly resilient, you should treat it carefully and consistently if you want it to continue.

> **A Researcher's Perspective: Sleep Regressions Are Not Inevitable**
>
> Sleep regressions are concepts that I do not use and do not agree with. If you assist a child to learn high-quality sleep skills early in life, those patterns are stable and much easier to maintain. They are less likely to be disrupted by normal variations in life.
>
> What people are saying is that at a particular age, they commonly observe that babies become unsettled. A well-known example is of course the four-month sleep regression.
>
> What is happening here is that the child is still largely milk fed but has outgrown milk as their only source of nutrition. They become hungry and begin to awaken overnight looking for extra feeds.
>
> The way to prevent this is to begin solids early enough and to allow the baby to guide the parents as to how rapidly to increase

volumes. Because my consulting has a focus on high-quality nutrition, I rarely if ever see families who experience "sleep regressions."

—Brian Symon, M.D.

Transitioning from the Swaddle

Now that you've successfully reached the end of the Dream Feed Method, give yourself a beat before you change anything. There's no rush, and the stability of achieving full nighttime sleep is an incredible accomplishment that you should just enjoy for a few weeks.

Many babies, sometime between the fifth and sixth month, will teach themselves how to turn over. Before that happens, you'll want them transitioned out of the swaddle. We'll encourage you to break up the transition into a few discrete steps.

Start by transitioning to a one-arm swaddle just during naps. Allow your baby to become accustomed to having access to one arm. But only do so during daytime naps, where the cost of the nap not going well won't ruin your entire night.

Once your baby feels comfortable with a one-arm swaddle during the day, you can introduce it at night, switching arms every other night.

After a few weeks of just one arm, or faster if you so choose, use the swaddle to snugly wrap around your baby's core, leaving both arms free. The small amount of pressure will provide a feeling of comfort, while your baby now has full access to his arms.

Finally, remove the swaddle completely and switch over to something like a sleep sack.

The whole process of transitioning from a full swaddle to a sleep sack can be done slowly over a month. And feel free, at any point, to take a step back if it's causing too much discomfort and tears.

Transitioning from a Nighttime Pacifier

If you got to 12 hours with the use of a nighttime pacifier, you probably shudder at the thought of not using it. Since that little pacifier has probably now been used hundreds of times to quietly soothe your baby, you don't like to think of the alternative.

For some babies, you won't actually need to transition away from a pacifier. They may use it to fall asleep, but when they wake up in the middle of the night, they don't need it back. If that's the case with your baby, you're fine. There's nothing else you need to do. There's nothing intrinsically wrong with the pacifier use, the only problem is if you're needed to retrieve it.

Becoming a pacifier-retriever is no good. It establishes a pattern where your baby is reliant on you to "save the day" when he wakes without his pacifier. Obviously, no parent wants to continue to be awakened in the middle of the night to retrieve the pacifier, and additionally, your baby starts to reinforce an expectation that can get worse over time.

So how do you transition? Once again, work with the time periods where things are the easiest. So if you're using a pacifier during daytime naps, start by removing daytime nap use. You can handle a bad nap in the middle of the day much better than you can handle an upset baby at 4:00 a.m. If you're using a pacifier to put the baby down at 7:00 p.m., you will need to wean your baby off that reliance, as well.

One nice thing to do is to help your baby learn how to use his own thumb. With arms that have better coordination and the transition away from a swaddle, your baby can now develop this new soothing technique that still utilizes his sucking reflex.

Some babies will develop it naturally, but if yours doesn't, simply guide his thumb to his mouth. And if he resists, use your own finger to allow him to see that the same relaxed sensation occurs sucking on a finger as it did on a pacifier. And then try again with his finger the next night.

A Pediatrician's Perspective: Turning the Baby's Thumb into a Pacifier

"Pacifier" literally means peacemaker. Giving baby something to suck on will often bring peace to both baby and parents. You can actually help your baby learn to suck his hand or thumb. These are "handier" than pacifiers. They are warm, soft, and easily available. They don't fall on the floor, they are just the right size for baby's mouth, and they don't obstruct the nose or need to be clipped on with a cord. Babies feel more in control of their hands.

—William Sears, M.D., *The Baby Sleep Book*

Joining Another Sibling in the Same Room

The transition to another sibling's room also invokes fear in many parents. At the very best, you assume there's going be a lowest common denominator effect in which both siblings get the least amount of sleep that either individual could obtain. And even just 30 to 60 minutes less sleep per night can have a pretty big impact on everyone's crankiness the next day. In the worst-case scenario, your babies have dramatically different sleep patterns. And you're concerned that they'll both keep each other up at different times.

The reality is many children learn how to sleep in the same room together. And depending upon your housing situation, there might not be a choice. So our overall guidance is to just go for it. In general, it's better to first get to a stable 12-hour sleep period in the most controlled environment possible. If you can wait until after your youngest has finished the Dream Feed Method and then transfer your good sleeper to a room with a sibling, it should work out just fine.

But even if you're doing sleep training with another child in the room, you'll be impressed by how resilient everyone can be. In general, babies aren't awakened by other noises; they wake because their bellies are empty. And the work that you're doing to teach good sleep habits and keep their bellies full can actually be done in a pretty wide variety of environments.

One trick that's worked well is separating the bedtime routines. If you have an older child who has a very different bedtime routine and your infant, who's got a fairly fragile process, just separate them. Let your older child have a special period of time in mommy and daddy's bed reading books and singing songs, and let the infant's go-to-sleep process be in a quiet, controlled space in the room.

A lot of parents fear this step. The end result is actually that you get to watch how quickly your children become best friends. Older siblings are incredibly loving and protective of their younger siblings from a very early age. And having the baby in their room is a special opportunity that makes both less lonely.

Traveling with Your Baby

If you're still progressing toward full dusk till dawn sleeping, try as much as possible to reduce your travel. It's just so hard to maintain your progress when you can't control the environment the way you can at home. After you have successfully reached those 12-hour nights, traveling is one of the great perks to having a successfully sleep-trained baby, because it won't be nearly as painful on either you or your baby.

Here are a few tips and tricks to ensuring that traveling with your newborn goes as smoothly as possible:

Do everything you can to duplicate the sleep environment at home. Bring a bassinet or a pack-and-play and place it in the darkest, quietest space you can find. Bring a white noise machine and portable blackout curtains if you're traveling during the summer months. They can usually be affixed with Velcro or suction cups, and it's a small price to pay to ensure that your baby falls asleep easily and stays asleep.

If you're traveling across time zones, your baby can actually change time zones and revert back fairly easy. So, if you move over one time zone, you can put your baby down at what will effectively feel like 6:00 p.m. instead of 7:00 p.m. The key is to repeat the entire go-to-bed process you do on normal nights at home. Run through the whole routine of turning the lights low, feeding in a dark room, etc. Your baby won't notice that you're earlier. These routine-oriented cues for sleep will be more important than an extra hour or two of tiredness.

Similarly, if your time zone moves in the other direction, you can put your baby down at what will feel like an hour later, and she'll stay up that whole time as long as you delay the going-to-sleep process by an hour as well.

If anything, the ability to shift time zones proves just how important consistency is to creating healthy sleep cues, because it is the sleep cues that are far more important than actual tiredness.

Once you get home, whether things progressed smoothly or not, simply jump right back into your normal routine, and you should find that your baby is able to adjust smoothly.

The only thing to be really careful about is letting the inconsistencies of travel continue once you've gotten home. For instance, sometimes sleeping away from home is kind of a disaster. Your baby was sick. The environment was too loud. For whatever reason, you had to go into survival mode. You did a lot of middle of the night soothing and off-schedule feedings.

That's still okay. Just make sure you go back to your previous routines once you get home. If prior to the trip, your baby was never fed at 4:00 a.m., but then received 4:00 a.m. feedings during the trip, be extra diligent in removing the 4:00 a.m. feedings once you get home. It may take a night or two of adjustment on your baby's part to get back to the consistency you had before the trip.

When Your Baby Is Sick

This section is probably so obvious it doesn't need to be written. But sometimes people take the rigidity of sleep training too far.

When your baby is sick, just comfort your baby.

Don't worry about sleep training. Don't worry about making progress or losing progress. You can't disrupt months of patterns in a couple of nights of comforting. And frankly, your baby is not going to learn anything about self-soothing while he's sick anyway.

One thing you do have to be careful about is getting back on track after your baby gets better. You don't want to introduce new patterns while your baby is sick and then keep them going long term. There will be a bit more crying when you return to your normal sleep routines and your baby relearns to soothe himself. However, it should be short-lived if you've been doing the Dream Feed Method diligently. You shouldn't have more than 15 minutes of crying before your baby goes back to soothing himself.

Lastly, doing a great job with sleep training early on is the single best thing you can do in advance of your baby getting sick. Healthy sleep habits give him the rest he needs to fight off these brand new infections his body is experiencing for the first time.

When Your Baby Is Teething

If you've done the Dream Feed Method right from the start, here is the best piece of news we can give you: your baby will already learn to sleep from dusk till dawn before he starts teething. And so, in most cases, he will sleep right through the discomfort of teething!

It's actually amazing to think that most parents try to do sleep training between the fourth and ninth months when teething is at its worst. Most babies haven't learned how to self-soothe, and now they have this additional new pain to endure. It's just too much for them to handle, and parents can't bear the thought of their baby crying in pain at night and not being comforted.

If you've started later and the discomfort from teething is waking your baby up, there's not a great solution on what to do. Some parents will choose the Tylenol route. Discuss that option with your pediatrician and make your own decision. We don't have a strong recommendation for or against.

Some parents will choose to comfort their baby. In general, we have found that it doesn't really work and that the time spent comforting just prolongs the period in which your baby is awake. It certainly slows down any sleep training progress. If you do choose to go that route during teething, just be mindful of whether it's successful in getting your baby back down to sleep.

Most importantly, start early with the Dream Feed Method, and this will be one of the challenges that won't even apply to you. Your baby will sleep right through teething, and you'll all be happier for it.

Acknowledgements

Special thank you to the family and friends of Jana Hartzell. Proceeds from this book will go to The Jana Hartzell Foundation, which supports the prenatal and postnatal education of all mothers of all income levels. Learn more at www.dreamfeedmethod.com/janahartzell

And thank you to Laurie and Josh Olshansky for your support in helping make this tribute to our beloved Jana reach mothers and fathers everywhere.

Grateful acknowledgement is made for the permission to use the following:

Excerpt(s) from SECRETS OF THE BABY WHISPERER: HOW TO CALM, CONNECT, AND COMMUNICATE WITH YOUR BABY by Tracy Hogg, copyright © 2001 by Tracy Hogg Enterprises, Inc. Used by permission of Ballantine Books, an imprint of Random House, a division of Penguin Random House, LLC. All rights reserved.

Excerpt(s) from BRINGING UP BÉBÉ: ONE AMERICAN MOTHER DISCOVERS THE WISDOM OF FRENCH PARENTING by Pamela Druckerman, copyright © 2012 by Pamela Druckerman. Used by permission of Penguin Press, an imprint of Penguin Publishing Group, a division of Penguin Random House, LLC. All rights reserved.

Six excerpts from pp. 39, 50-1, 69, 72-3, 91, 168-9 from THE HAPPIEST BABY GUIDE TO GREAT SLEEP by Harvey Karp, M.D. Copyright © 2012 by THB Media, LLC. Reprint by permission of HarperCollins Publishers.

Excerpts from THE SCIENCE OF MOM: A RESEARCH-BASED GUIDE TO YOUR BABY'S FIRST YEAR Copyright © 2015 by Alice Callahan, PhD. Used by permission of Johns Hopkins University Press.

Excerpt(s) from TWELVE HOURS' SLEEP BY TWELVE WEEKS OLD: A STEP-BY-STEP PLAN FOR BABY SLEEP SUCCESS by Suzy Giordano, with Lisa Abidin, copyright © 2006 by Suzy Giordano and Lisa Abidin. Used by permission of Dutton, an imprint of Penguin Publishing Group, a division of Penguin Random House, LLC. All rights reserved.

References

American Academy of Pediatrics. *Caring for Your Baby and Young Child.* New York: Bantam, 2009.

Blau, Melinda, and Tracy Hogg. *Secrets of the Baby Whisperer.* Los Angeles, CA: Atria Books, 2006.

Callahan, Alice. *The Science of Mom.* Baltimore: Johns Hopkins UP, 2015.

Cronenwett, Linda, Therese Stukel, Margaret Kearney, Jane Barrett, Chandice Covington, Kristen Del Monte, Robert Reinhardt, and Laurie Rippe. "Single Daily Bottle Use in the Early Weeks Postpartum and Breast-Feeding Outcomes." *The Journal of Pediatrics* 90 (1992):760–766.

Dowling, Donna, and Warinee Thanattherakul. "Nipple Confusion, Alternative Feeding Methods, and Breast-Feeding Supplementation." *Newborn and Infant Nursing Reviews.* 1(4) (December 2001): 217–23.

Druckerman, Pamela. *Bringing Up Bébé.* New York: Penguin, 2014.

Ferber, Richard. *Solve Your Child's Sleep Problems.* Wichita, KS: Fireside, 1985.

Fisher, Chloe, and Sally Inch. "Letter to the Editor." *Journal of Pediatrics* 129 (1) (July 1996): 174–75.

Giordano, Suzy. *Twelve Hours' Sleep by Twelve Weeks Old.* London: TarcherPerigee, 2006.

Howorth, Claire. "The Goddess Myth: Motherhood is Hard to Get Wrong. So Why Do So Many Moms Feel So Bad About Themselves." *Time Magazine* Oct 2017.

Karp, Harvey. *The Happiest Baby Guide to Great Sleep.* Harper Collins, 2013

Neifert, Marianne, Ruth Lawrence, and Joy Seacat. "Nipple Confusion: Toward a Formal Definition." *The Journal of Pediatrics* 126 (6) (June 1995): S125–29.

Pinilla, Teresa, and Leann Birch. "Help Me Make It through the Night: Behavioral Entrainment of Breast-fed Infants' Sleep Patterns." *Pediatrics* 91 (2) (February 1993): 436–44.

Sadeh, Avi. *Sleeping Like a Baby: A Sensitive and Sensible Approach to Solving Your Child's Sleep Problems.* New Haven, CT: Yale UP, 2001.

Schubiger, Gregor, Uwe Schwarz, Otmar Tonz, and Neonatal Study Group. "UNICEF/ WHO Baby-Friendly Hospital Initiative: Does the Use of Bottles and Pacifiers in the Neonatal Nursery Prevent Successful Breastfeeding?" *European Journal of Pediatrics* 156(11) (1997): 874–77.

Sears, William. *The Baby Book.* New York: Little Brown and Company, 2008.

Sears, William. *The Baby Sleep Book.* New York: Little Brown and Company, 2005.

Symon, Brian. *Silent Nights: Overcoming Sleep Problems in Babies and Children.* London: Oxford UP, 2005.

Symon, Brian. *Your Baby Manual ... for Optimal Sleep, Feeding, and Growth in Babies and Children.* Minneapolis, MN: Two Harbors Press, 2016.

Symon, Brian, John E. Marley, James Martin, and Emily Norman. "Effect of a Consultation Teaching Behavior Modification on Sleep Performance in Infants: A Randomized Controlled Trial." *The Medical Journal of Australia* 182 (5) (March 2005): 215–18.

Volkovich, Ella, Hamutal Ben-Zion, Daphna Karny, Gal Meiri, and Liat Tikotzky. "Sleep Patterns of Co-Sleeping and Solitary Sleeping Infants and Mothers: A Longitudinal Study." *Sleep Medicine* 16 (11) (November 2015): 1305–12.

Weissbluth, Marc. *Healthy Sleep Habits, Happy Child.* New York: Ballantine Books, 1999.

World Health Organization (WHO). "Innocenti Declaration," accessed January 25, 2017, http://www.who.int/about/agenda/health_development/events/innocenti_declaration_1990.pdf.

World Health Organization (WHO)/UNICEF. "Ten Steps to Successful Breastfeeding," accessed January 25, 2017, http://www.tensteps.org.

Index

A

Aicardi, Dr. Eileen 14, 36, 38, 41, 49, 60, 103, 127, 166, 183, 201
American Academy of Pediatrics 89, 94, 177, 195
Author's Perspective
  Bébé's La Pause 164
  Don't interrupt sleep for nighttime changes 126
  Fed is best 54
  Just be close 176
  Just Take It Easy 91
  Putting baby down while awake 194
  Quiet nighttime feedings 69
  Swaddling doesn't hurt hips 168

B

Baby shusher 189
Back to Birth Weight 90
Back-to-Sleep 88
Bad sleeper 36
Bassinet 190
Bedtime 108
Birch, Leann 36, 68
Blackout curtains 187
Blau, Melinda 65
Bottle-feeding 2, 60
Breastfeeding 2, 29, 44, 51, 59, 60, 92
Breast is Best 29
Breathing monitor 191
Burp 110

C

Callahan, Dr. Alice 163
Caroline 119
Cluster Feed 106
Colic 109, 111
co-sleeping 89
Co-sleeping 2, 28, 68, 177, 179, 180
Crib 190
Cry-and-respond 68
Crying 63, 124, 128, 164, 195
Cry-it-out 41, 68, 69, 71, 76, 124